"We are made for complementarity. I have gifts you do not; and you have gifts that I do not. So we need each other to become fully human."
   — from *An African Prayer Book* by Archbishop
      Desmond Tutu

"Marriage is the golden ring in a chain whose beginning is a glance and whose ending is an eternity."
   — Kahlil Gibran

"There is one and only one/who will give the air/from his failing lungs/for my body's mend/And that one is my love."
   — from *Many and More* by Maya Angelou

"Love is the key to the solution of the problems of the world."
   — from the December 1968 Nobel Prize Lecture
      by Dr. Martin Luther King Jr.

TAMARA NIKURADSE is the author of *My Mother Had a Dream*, as well as several other successful inspirational books. A graduate of Harvard Business School, she graduated magna cum laude from Bowdoin College with a degree in African-American studies. She is a marketing executive at Gillette.

African-American Wedding Readings

O O

EDITED BY

TAMARA NIKURADSE

A PLUME BOOK

PLUME

Published by the Penguin Group

Penguin Putnam Inc., 375 Hudson Street, New York, New York 10014, U.S.A.

Penguin Books Ltd, 27 Wrights Lane, London W8 5TZ, England

Penguin Books Australia Ltd, Ringwood, Victoria, Australia

Penguin Books Canada Ltd, 10 Alcorn Avenue, Toronto, Ontario, Canada M4V 3B2

Penguin Books (N.Z.) Ltd, 182–190 Wairau Road, Auckland 10, New Zealand

Penguin Books Ltd, Registered Offices: Harmondsworth, Middlesex, England

Published by Plume, an imprint of Dutton NAL, a member of Penguin Putnam Inc.
Previously published in a Dutton edition.

First Plume Printing, January, 1999

10 9 8 7 6 5 4 3 2 1

Ⓟ REGISTERED TRADEMARK—MARCA REGISTRADA

The Library of Congress has catalogued the Dutton edition as follows:

African-American wedding readings / edited by Tamara Nikuradse.
     p.   cm.
  ISBN 0-525-94403-6 (hc)
  ISBN 0-452-28023-0 (pbk)
  1. Afro-Americans—Marriage customs and rites. 2. Weddings—United States—Literary
collections. 3. Marriage—United States—Literary collections. I. Nikuradse, Tamara.
E185.86.A33445 1998
392.5'08996073-dc21
                       97-28998
                       CIP
Printed in the United States of America
Original hardcover design by Leonard Telesca

DEDICATION

Peace and blessings to the bride and groom—may
the love expressed in this book be but a teaspoonful
from the ocean of your love for one another. Here's
to an eternity of happiness together.

Contents

Introduction

Love is the light of the world.

—*Paul Laurence Dunbar*

*A*fter ten years of living together, in 1992 my significant other, Scott Matthews, and I decided that we should finally tie the knot. Rather than having an elaborate, formal, and expensive wedding, we chose to escape to Bermuda with thirty of our closest friends and relatives in tow. The wedding would be a dream come true for both of us.

Since the age of sixteen, I had always envisioned my wedding on a beach. I wanted the sun and the sky to be the stained glass window with a choir of waves crashing on a coral beach. The warm pink sand would replace cold, wooden pews while the swaying palm trees would substitute as exquisite floral arrangements. The minister would officiate in traditional clergy garb from the waist up, but from the waist down he would be in shorts or she would be in a sarong.

Similarly, Scott had dreams of a wedding on the tranquil isle of Bermuda. Although Scott is not Bermudian by birth, spiritually (he would argue) he is. Scott's incredible admiration for the island, its culture, and the Bermudian people had been nurtured in him since he

first started making annual pilgrimages to Bermuda as a young boy. He wanted to share all the treasures of Bermuda with his most cherished family members, dearest friends, and loving bride-to-be during a week-long wedding celebration culminating in a picturesque beachside wedding!

Given that the company I was working for at the time was relocating, all of my attention was focused on securing a new job rather than planning our wedding. Likewise, Scott was immersed in his new job, having just graduated from business school a few months earlier. Fortunately, my future mother-in-law and dearest friend, Gail Matthews, planned the entire wedding affair with little assistance from Scott, my mother (who was taking care of my ailing father in Los Angeles), or myself. Although Gail never once set foot on the island during the entire wedding planning process, she single-handedly selected the menu, musician (a one-man band with a Casio keyboard), flowers, transportation, accommodations, and photographer. She even had a little talk with God to ensure that the weather would be perfect on our wedding day—sunny with temperatures in the seventies and a cool ocean breeze.

Gail had repeatedly encouraged us to write wedding vows or select some inspirational readings on love and marriage to be shared with our guests during the wedding ceremony. Unfortunately, our limited search for the perfect words to express our deepest feelings for each other was futile. I could not find a collection of wedding readings that incorporated the richness of my African, West Indian, and African-American heritage. Although I discovered books of wedding readings filled with beautiful works from Shakespeare to Dickinson, there were no collections of wedding readings from Wheatley to Giovanni that captured the soul and emotions of my unconditional love for Scott.

Given how quickly the wedding day descended upon us, neither Scott nor I had the time required to search through volumes of poetry and prose in the library or bookstore. To our regret, we opted not to have our guests participate in the wedding ceremony by reciting spe-

cially selected readings. And we chose not to exchange more meaningful vows beyond the traditional "Do you take this woman...." What could have been a perfect wedding day was indelibly tarnished by these omissions.

Years later, after I had practically forgotten about the futile search to find a volume of African-inspired wedding readings, my editor, Jennifer Moore, approached me with such a book idea. Why not develop a book of wedding readings filled with inspirational writings on love and marriage from around the African diaspora? This concept for such a book was clearly long overdue. I couldn't help but kick myself for not having started this project over five years ago!

Gathered within these pages is a collection of inspiring works from all corners of the African diaspora—from Africa to the West Indies and through the Americas. The readings are as diverse as all the great peoples, cultures, and timeless traditions that have enriched the African experience since the beginning of time. This collection of readings pays homage to the unconditional love and strong tradition of marriage in many African-based communities throughout history. Many of the readings within the collection go beyond the traditional Western concept of romantic love to a more spiritual level of love that is nurtured and refined through years of turmoil and bliss.

Although this collection of wedding readings is barely the tip of the iceberg, for those of you who do not have the luxury of time to spend months in a library or bookstore searching for that perfect reading, this collection is a good start. I encourage you to use the readings as an inspiration to write your own special vows or simply to expand upon them by adding a few heartfelt words to make the readings more personal. The acknowledgments section in the back of this collection is an excellent source of books for those of you who want more.

By incorporating readings found in this collection as well as African-inspired traditions, your wedding ceremony will not only be a

celebration of your love but also a celebration of your rich heritage for all to rejoice in. May your wedding day and all the days after be blessed with unconditional love for each other. Congratulations.

A Note on How to Use this Book

*T*his collection is organized to follow the evolution of a marriage: starting with a couple's engagement, progressing through the wedding, and culminating with a wedding reaffirmation.

I extend an invitation to you to use any one of these readings to make your wedding even more special. Please feel free to tailor the readings to your ceremony. It's easy to make a few minor changes that do not disrupt the meaning of the works. Here's how . . . You may want to replace a name in a reading with the name of your loved one (or your loved one's nickname). Write in longhand one of the readings that has a special meaning and send it to your loved one in the form of a love note. Place the short quotes on wedding invitations, programs, or favors. You may also want your reader to preface the reading with a brief introduction so your wedding guests understand the significance of the words. Please feel free to use any of the following introductions to preface a reading.

[The bride] and [the groom] offer this definition of love . . .

Through this reading, [the bride] pledges her undying devotion to [her groom] . . .

Here is a voice from the last century speaking to [the bride] and [the groom] about living and loving . . .

[The groom] wishes to acknowledge the love of our ancestors, who have bequeathed to us all the strength of their love. This inheritance gives [the groom] strength to proclaim his love in the form of this reading . . .

[The groom] has searched libraries near and far for the words to describe what [the bride] has brought into his life. He offers this reading to frame his thoughts, but counsels, these words are but a teaspoonful from the ocean of his love for [his bride] . . .

[The groom] selected this poem written in the nineteenth century to tell us how he feels when he gazes upon [the bride] . . .

[The groom] wishes to bestow upon [his bride] the treasures from his heart, and may this reading be a symbol of this treasure . . .

This is your new beginning together, united before all of us, united in the eyes of God, united in your love for one another . . .

The loved ones who have gathered before you to bask in the glory and righteousness of your love have a dream to share with you, a dream we pray is realized in your new world together . . .

Many, many years from now, we wish you both the divine love that you feel today, and we wish that your anniversary songs in years to come be mighty songs of love.

[The groom] has bestowed unto me the privilege of reading this poem that speaks from his heart. It is dedicated to [the bride].

Love Is . . .

Love stretches your heart and makes you big inside.

—From *Jubilee* by Margaret Walker

*A*fter the announcement of your engagement, you probably breathed a sigh of relief because it was now official: You have found your life's partner and will spend the rest of your life with this phenomenal person. During this engagement, the love you share with your fiancé somehow seems to have blossomed even more than you ever thought possible. Finally, each of you can let down your guard and truly be yourselves without the fear of losing the one you love because of some little imperfection (usually only noticeable to your friends).

With the onset of the engagement not only do you feel a more passionate love for each other but also a deeper level of commitment. Each of you has a much greater sense of obligation for the health, happiness, and welfare of the other person than you ever had before. Now when you make a decision you must think of the impact of that decision on your fiancé. You have quickly learned the fine art of negotiation and compromise. No longer are you thinking of yourself first but of your partnership together.

How can you possibly describe this new level of love in just a few

words? In this section, I attempt to uncover some of the meanings of this new level of love as defined throughout the African diaspora in prose and poetry. For example, Dr. Martin Luther King Jr. explores the Greek words for *love*, which seem to more aptly describe the different types of love than is possible with the limited English language. Similarly, Malcolm X explores love beyond what he defines as the Western definition of love—lust—to what comprises the beauty found in a woman, a beauty that never fails.

Finally, I would encourage you to discuss with your parents their definition of love and perhaps use that definition in your ceremony, because you are the fruit borne from their love, just like your children will be the living testimony to your love. These passages can also be read at an engagement party—by a family member, a friend, or you or your fiancé.

God is love, and those who abide in love abide in God, and God abides in them. Love has been perfected among us in this: that we may have boldness on the day of judgment, because as he is, so are we in this world. There is no fear in love, but perfect love casts out fear; for fear has to do with punishment, and whoever fears has not reached perfection in love. We love because he first loved us.

—John (4:16–19) Holy Bible: New Revised Standard Version

"Stella, will you marry me?"

I turn away to look over at the swimming pool for no particular reason except to maybe catch my breath and then I look up at the black sky that has absolutely no stars which is like totally perfect because they are not necessary and so I ponder this thought this notion this gesture this whole idea for a few more seconds and then I smile at Winston and press my lips softly into his and I do love this man I do I do but I look at him one more time to make sure he's like for real and when I see that he is I take a deep breath to make sure I am real and Stella girl accept the fact that you finally got something you wanted, that it's okay to enjoy him this moment go on and make this move feel this groove fool go ahead jump dive in deep fly swirl girl you have earned this you deserve this you can take this to the bank, so when I like hear all this advice and stuff being given to me by this mature-in-the-middle-of-her-life woman who knows what day it is what time it is and whose name happens to be the same as mine I am like totally sold swayed convinced so I just go ahead and drape my arms around this beautiful man named Winston Shakespeare and I say, "Okay!"

—From *How Stella Got Her Groove Back* by Terry McMillan

Some people forget that love is
tucking you in and kissing you "Good night"
no matter how young or old you are

Some people don't remember that love is
listening and laughing and asking questions
no matter what your age

Few recognize that love is
commitment   responsibility   no fun at all
unless

Love is
You and me
　　—"Love Is" by Nikki Giovanni

Love will open your mind like the chaste leaf in the morning
when the sun first touches it.
　　—Wole Soyinka

　　　To be in love
Is to touch things with a lighter hand.

In yourself you stretch, you are well.

You look at things
Through his eyes.
　　　A Cardinal is red.
　　　A sky is blue.
Suddenly you know he knows too.

He is not there but
You know you are tasting together
The winter, or light spring weather.

His hand to take your hand is overmuch.
Too much to bear.

You cannot look in his eyes
Because your pulse must not say
What must not be said.

When he
Shuts a door—
Is not there—
Your arms are water.

And you are free
With a ghastly freedom.

You are the beautiful half
Of a golden hurt.

You remember and covet his mouth,
To touch, to whisper on.

Oh when to declare
Is certain Death!

Oh when to apprize
Is to mesmerize,

To see fall down, the Column of Gold,
Into the commonest ash.

    —"To Be in Love" by Gwendolyn Brooks

Love triumphs.
The white and green of love beside a lake,
And the proud majesty of love in tower or balcony;
Love in a garden or in the desert untrodden,
Love is our lord and master.
It is not a wanton decay of the flesh,
Nor the crumbling of desire
When desire and self are wrestling;
Nor is it flesh that takes arms against the spirit.
Love rebels not.

It only leaves the trodden way of ancient destinies for the
    sacred grove,
To sing and dance its secret to eternity.
Love is youth with chains broken,
Manhood made free from the sod,
And womanhood warmed by the flame
And shining with the light of heaven deeper than our heaven.
Love is a distant laughter in the spirit.
It is a wild assault that hushes you to your awakening.
It is a new dawn upon the earth,
A day not yet achieved in your eyes or mine,
But already achieved in its own greater heart.

Brothers, my brothers,
The bride comes from the heart of dawn,
And the bridegroom from the sunset.
There is a wedding in the valley.
A day too vast for recording.
    —From *The Earth Gods* by Kahlil Gibran

Love is the soothing voice of gods
    To which men ever list.
Love is the ease of soul's travail
    And sorrow's alchemist.
    —"Love" by Joseph S. Cotter Jr.

the world is not a pleasant place
to be without
someone to hold and be held by

a river would stop
its flow if only
a stream were there
to receive it

an ocean would never laugh
if clouds weren't there
to kiss her tears

the world is not
a pleasant place to be without
someone
    —"The World Is Not a Pleasant Place to Be" by Nikki Giovanni

I hope you will remember me now just as same as you did when I was there with you because my mind is with you night and day. The love that I bear for you in my breast is greater than I thought it was. If I had thought I had so much love for you I don't think I ever left, being I have escape and fled into a land of freedom. I can but stop and look over my past life and say what a fool I was for staying in bondage as long. My dear wife, I don't want you to get married before you send me some letters, because I never shall get married until I see you again. My mind don't deceive and it appears to me as if I shall see you again.

—Excerpt from a letter by Samuel Washington Johnson, an escaped slave, to his enslaved wife

It lifts the poor man from his cell
    To fortune's bright alcove;
Its mighty sway few, few can tell,
Mid envious foes it conquers ill;
    There's nothing half like love.

Ye weary strangers, void of rest,
    Who late through life have strove,
Like the late bird which seeks its nest,
If you would hence in truth be blest,
    Light on the bough of love.

The vagrant plebeian, void of friends,
    Constrain'd through wilds to rove,
On this his safety whole depends,
One faithful smile his trouble ends,
    A smile of constant love.

Thus did a captured wretch complain,
    Imploring heaven above,
Till one with sympathetic pain,
Flew to his arms and broke the chain,
    And grief took flight from love.

Let clouds of danger rise and roar,
    And hope's firm pillars move,
With storms behind and death before,
O grant me this, I crave no more,
    There's nothing half like love.

When nature wakes soft pity's coo
    The hawk deserts the dove,
Compassion melts the creature through,
With palpitations felt by few,
    The wrecking throbs of love.

Let surly discord take its flight
    From wedlock's peaceful grove,
While union breaks the arm of fight,
With darkness swallow'd up in light,
    O what is there like love.
    —"The Powers of Love" by George Moses Horton

Perhaps it was more happiness than love, though the one cannot exist without the other. . . . Happiness and passion. Maybe
that is what love really is.
    —Camara Laye

It is the color of light,
the shape of sound
high in the evergreens.

It lies suspended in hills,
a blue line in a red
sky.

I am looking at sound.
I am hearing the brightness
of high bluffs and almond
trees. I am
tasting the wilderness of lakes,
rivers, and streams
caught in an angle
of song.

I am remembering water
that glows in the dawn,
and motion tumbled
in earth, life hidden in mounds.

I am dancing a bright
beam of light.

I am remembering love.
   —"Lyric: I Am Looking at Music" by Pinkie Gordon Lane

Love is not love demanding all, itself
Withholding aught; love's is the nobler way
Of courtesy, that will not feast aware
That the beloved hungers, nor drink unless
The cup be shared down to the last sweet dregs.
Renunciatory never was the thorn
To crown love with, but *prodigal* and *proud*!
Too proud to rest the debtor of the one
Dear passion most it dotes upon, always
Love rehabilitates unto the end.
So let it be with us; the perfect faith
We each to other swear this moment leaves
Our scales harmonious, neither wanting found
Though weighed in such strict balances. So let
It be with us always. I am too proud
To owe you one caress; you must not drop
Beholden to my favor for one least
Endearing term. Should you reveal some stretch
Of sky to me, let me revive some note
Of music lost to you. This is love's way,
That where a heart is asked gives back a heart
　—"Love's Way" by Countee Cullen

By the summer of 1962, I had been at Fort Devens for eighteen months and was due for orders. They arrived in August; I was going to South Vietnam.... All Alma wanted to know was what my orders meant for us. I told her that the Vietnam assignment was for one year, and that I had no idea where I would be sent afterward. I told her that I cared deeply for her, and I hoped she would write me often. Her reply floored me: "I'm not going to write to you." If she was going to be only a pen pal, she said, "we might as well end it now." She was almost twenty-five, Alma went on, and she had no intention of sitting around waiting to see if I was still in the picture a year from now.

I drove back to Devens dejected. Her reaction forced me to ask myself something I had not faced so far. How much did this woman mean to me?

That night, I lay in my bunk taking emotional inventory of the relationship. Alma Johnson was beautiful, intelligent, refined, and fun to be with, and, all too rare in a romance, she was my friend. She came from a fine family, got along with my circle of friends, and was even a great cook. I knew that she loved me, and I loved her. My folks loved her too. What was I waiting for? Alma had everything I would ever want in a wife. I was a jerk for not acting before she got away. This nonsense that if the Army wanted you to have a wife it would have issued you one had to go.

I could barely wait to drive back to Boston the next day and ask her to marry me. Thank God, she said yes.

—Excerpt from *My American Journey* by Colin L. Powell

It takes a smart woman to fall in love with a good man.
　—From *Having Our Say* by Sadie and Bessie Delany

How much living have you done?
From it the patterns that you weave
Are imaged:
Your own life is your totem pole,
Your yard of cloth,
Your living.

How much loving have you done?
How full and free your giving?
For living is but loving
And loving only giving.
　—"The Poet Speaks" by Georgia Douglas Johnson

The greatest thing about love is that when it's there,
you know it.
　—Bill Cosby

8

Four winds and seven seas have called me friend,
And countless roads have known my restless feet;
Deep crystal springs and pollened buds were sweet
For sustenance their princely fare to lend,
While nameless birds from grove and blossomed bend
Deluged my soul with song; if it were meet
To love Life so, then Love will but complete
My joy, for Life with Love can never end.
Love, I have heard the sweet of your voice, have seen
You pass the dawn-flushed singing hills between;
Now suppliant I kneel and pray you show
The mercied sceptre favored Esther saw;
The dawn in me has broke, and well I know
That Love is king and creed and Persian law.
   —"From Life to Love" by Countee Cullen

♥

I love Betty. She's the only woman I ever even thought about loving. And she's one of the very few—four women—whom I have ever trusted. The thing is, Betty's a good Muslim woman and wife. You see, Islam is the only religion that gives both husband and wife a true understanding of what love is. The Western "love" concept, you take it apart, it really is lust. But love transcends just the physical. Love is disposition, behavior, attitude, thoughts, likes, dislikes—these things make a beautiful woman, a beautiful wife. This is the beauty that never fades. You find in your Western civilization that when a man's wife's physical beauty fails, she loses her attraction. But Islam teaches us to look into the woman, and teaches her to look into us.

　—From *The Autobiography of Malcolm X* by Malcolm X with Alex Haley

Love has no awareness of merit or demerit; it has no scale by which its portion may be weighed or measured. It does not seek to balance giving and receiving. Love loves; this is its nature.

　—Howard Thurman

@

Love hath the wings of the butterfly,
　　Oh, clasp him but gently,
Pausing and dipping and fluttering by
　　Inconsequently.
Stir not his poise with the breath of a sigh;
Love hath the wings of the butterfly.

Love hath the wings of the eagle bold,
　　Cling to him strongly—
What if the look of the world be cold,
　　And life go wrongly?
Rest on his pinions, for broad is their fold;
Love hath the wings of the eagle bold.

Love hath the voice of the nightingale,
　　Hearken his trilling—
List to his song when the moonlight is pale,—
　　Passionate, thrilling.
Cherish the lay, ere the lilt of it fail;
Love hath the voice of the nightingale.
　　—"Love's Phases" by Paul Laurence Dunbar

✿

　When you love you should not say, "God is in my heart," but
rather, "I am in the heart of God."
　　—From *The Prophet* by Kahlil Gibran

It is curious that in so rich a language as English there is only one word for all the different kinds of love. Martin said many times, though it bears repeating here, that the Greeks had three words for it! First there was *erōs*, which in Platonist philosophy meant the yearning of the soul for the divine and now has come to mean aesthetic or romantic love. *Philia* meant reciprocal love, as between friends or men and women. . . . The third kind of love was *agapē*. This meant understanding, redeeming goodwill toward all men. It was disinterested love in which the individual sought not his own good, but the good of his neighbor. It was not weak or passive, but love in action. Love of this sort is not sentimental; it is active. If you love you do something about that love.

—From *My Life with Martin Luther King Jr.* by Coretta Scott King

♦♦♦

Love is the key to the solution of the problems of the world.
—From the December 1968 Nobel Prize Lecture by Dr. Martin Luther King Jr.

≈

Love is patient and kind; love is not jealous or boastful; it is not arrogant or rude. Love does not insist on its own way; it is not irritable or resentful; it does not rejoice at wrong, but rejoices in the right. Love bears all things, believes all things, hopes all things, endures all things. Love never ends.
—I Corinthians (13:4–8a) New English Bible

Love is everlasting. Love is the activity of life, the active power in all of creation, present everywhere, at every moment, in exactly the same degree. We are sustained by love and couldn't separate ourselves from it even if we tried. Love binds us to God, to one another, yet allows us individuality at the same time. A loving relationship is a delicious thing, but it's not where love begins. A romantic relationship provides us with an opportunity to express love, but with or without a relationship, love exists in us and as us.

Love. We think about it, speak about it, celebrate it in song and dance. But we must move beyond the many clichés and abstract ways in which we refer to love. The great spiritual teacher Eric Butterworth, who has informed much of my thinking over the years, says we must personalize and practice what it means to be created in the image and likeness of God. He says we should "Note the logical implication of this. Each of us is created in and of love. God loves us. God is love in us. Each of us is the very activity of love. We have all the love we need to love everyone and everything."

—Excerpt from *In the Spirit* by Susan L. Taylor

TESTIMONIES OF LOVE:
A BRIDE'S WORDS FOR HER GROOM

When you love a man, he becomes more than a body. His physical limbs expand, and his outline recedes, vanishes. He is rich and sweet and right. He is part of the world, the atmosphere, the blue sky and the blue water.

—From *Report from Part One* by Gwendolyn Brooks

Other than the day you give birth, your wedding day is traditionally the happiest day of your life. If you are like most women, you have been dreaming about your wedding day since you were a little girl. As you listened to the fairy tale of Cinderella, you probably conjured up images of the handsome prince who would sweep you off your feet and take you to his castle in the sky. Over the years you and your girlfriends have imagined every detail of your wedding right down to the very first song you and your husband would dance to during the reception—even the song you and your father would share together.

As this long-awaited day quickly becomes reality, let's take some time to reflect on Prince Charming. Out of all the men in the universe, he was crowned Mr. Right. His smooth style, endless charm, quick wit, magnanimous heart, and big puppy dog eyes mesmerized you from day one. He was the one who made your knees wobble, made you feel

hot and bothered, made you forget about all your girlfriends, and made you realize that you wanted to spend every day of the rest of your life with him. Well that day has finally come. And now, in front of your closest friends and relatives, you will commit yourself eternally to him with God as your witness.

To help you express your love, devotion, and gratitude to your groom, why not select a reading such as "Devoted to You," which beautifully presents a woman's pledge of devotion to her man. You can use these selections as part of your vows.

For the mountains may depart
    and the hills be removed,
but my steadfast love shall not depart from you,
    and my covenant of peace shall not be removed,
    says the Lord, who has compassion on you.
        —Isaiah (54:10) Holy Bible: New Revised Standard Version

We are not lovers
because of the love
we make
but the love
we have

We are not friends
because of the laughs
we spend
but the tears
we save

I don't want to be near you
for the thoughts we share
but the words we never have
to speak

I will never miss you
because of what we do
but what we are
together
        —"A Poem of Friendship" by Nikki Giovanni

Walking with you
shuts off shivering.
Here we are.
Here we are.

I am with you to share and to bear and to care.

This is warm.
I want you happy, I want you warm.

Your Friend for our forever is what I am.
Your Friend in thorough thankfulness.

It is the evening of our love.
Evening is hale and whole.
Evening shall not go out.
Evening is comforting flame.
Evening is comforting flame.
　　—"Friend" by Gwendolyn Brooks

Sculpted from the clay of Africa,
first man in all the universe,
you were created in the image of a tree.
Transplanted now to foreign soil,
you are still wondrous in your towering vigor
and amplitude, and in the shade you give.

Tender birch or seasoned oak, mahogany or cedar,
baobab or ebony, you are the joy of a new Eden,
crested with leaves as varied
as fades and dreadlocks.

Your countenance, like rings of a stalwart trunk,
tells the unmatched story
of how you persevered and flourished
in spite of bitter storms.

Majestic man, enduring man of myriad visages,
continue to grow strong and tall
within the circle of my love.

   —"First Man" by Naomi Long Madgett

I will share and magnify your joys in life . . .
I will grow, love and support you . . .
I love, respect and enjoy you just as you are . . .
I adore you and will cherish you all the days of my life . . . and
   so it is!!!

   —From the wedding vows written by Ornetta Barber Dickerson to
Gregg Dickerson recited by Reverend O. C. Smith on February 24,
1990.

Other loves I have known.
One there was which struck suddenly,
Like a great stone
Plunging the waters of a quiet pool
It troubled my being with violent ecstasy . . .
Then easing gradually
It eddied away . . . was gone,
Lost in ever-widening ripples
Of calm, cool
Apathy.

Another came almost imperceptibly,
Like the subtle fragrance of a flower
Wind-scattered in Spring
It claimed my senses delicately;
Suffused me with yearning tenderness
For one enraptured hour . . .
Then being a thing
Infinitely too fragile to last,
At the very dawn of its budding
It passed.

I am glad, Dear One, that I have known
So much of vagrant love;
Each ephemeral travesty
Has but served to prove
That this which has grown
Oakwise with time,
Storm tested by you and me
Is, and ever shall be
The gift sublime,
The intransmutable verity.
   —"Proof" by Bessie Calhoun Bird

There are many and more
who would kiss my hand,
taste my lips,
to my loneliness lend
their bodies' warmth.

I have want of a friend.

There are few, some few,
who would give their names
and fortunes rich
or send first sons
to my ailing bed.

I have need of a friend.

There is one and only one
who will give the air
from his failing lungs
for my body's mend.

And that one is my love.
  —"Many and More" by Maya Angelou

His Love has been a joyous light
    That o'er her pathway smiled,
A fountain gushing ever new,
    Amid life's desert wild.
    From "The Slave Mother" by Francis Ellen Watkins Harper

The Song of Songs, which is Solomon's.
Let him kiss me with the kisses of his mouth!
For your love is better than wine,
    your anointing oils are fragrant,
your name is perfume poured out;
    therefore the maidens love you.
Draw me after you, let us make haste.
    The king has brought me into his chambers.
We will exult and rejoice in you;
    we will extol your love more than wine;
    rightly do they love you.

I am black and beautiful

.   .   .   .

I compare you, my love,
    to a mare among Pharaoh's chariots.
Your cheeks are comely with ornaments,
    your neck with strings of jewels.
We will make you ornaments of gold,
    studded with silver.

While the king was on his couch,
    my nard gave forth its fragrance.
My beloved is to me a bag of myrrh
    that lies between my breasts.
My beloved is to me a cluster of henna blossoms
    in the vineyards of En-gedi.

Ah, you are beautiful, my love;
    ah, you are beautiful;
    your eyes are doves.
Ah, you are beautiful, my beloved,
    truly lovely.

The voice of my beloved!
    Look, he comes,
leaping upon the mountains,
    bounding over the hills.
My beloved is like a gazelle
    or a young stag.
Look, there he stands
    behind our wall,
gazing in at the windows,
    looking through the lattice.
My beloved speaks and says to me:
"Arise, my love, my fair one,
    and come away;
for now the winter is past,
    the rain is over and gone.
The flowers appear on the earth;
    the time of singing has come,
and the voice of the turtledove
    is heard in our land.
The fig tree puts forth its figs,
    and the vines are in blossom;
    they give forth fragrance.
Arise, my love, my fair one,
    and come away.
O my dove, in the clefts of the rock,
    in the covert of the cliff,
let me see your face,

    let me hear your voice;
for your voice is sweet,
    and your face is lovely.
Catch us the foxes,
    the little foxes,

that ruin the vineyards—
    for our vineyards are in blossom."

My beloved is mine and I am his;
    he pastures his flock among the lilies.
Until the day breathes
    and the shadows flee,
turn, my beloved, be like a gazelle
    or a young stag on the cleft mountains.

. . . .

My beloved is all radiant and ruddy,
    distinguished among ten thousand.
His head is the finest gold;
    his locks are wavy,
    black as a raven.
His eyes are like doves
    beside springs of water,
bathed in milk,
    fitly set.
His cheeks are like beds of spices,
    yielding fragrance.
His lips are lilies,
    distilling liquid myrrh.
His arms are rounded gold,
    set with jewels.
His body is ivory work,
    encrusted with sapphires.
His legs are alabaster columns,
    set upon bases of gold.
His appearance is like Lebanon,
    choice as the cedars.
His speech is most sweet,
    and he is altogether desirable.
This is my beloved and this is my friend,

O daughters of Jerusalem.

.   .   .   .

I am my beloved's,
   and his desire is for me.
Come, my beloved,
   let us go forth into the fields,
   and lodge in the villages;
let us go out early to the vineyards,
   and see whether the vines have budded,
whether the grape blossoms have opened
   and the pomegranates are in bloom.
There I will give you my love.
The mandrakes give forth fragrance,
   and over our doors are all choice fruits,
new as well as old,
   which I have laid up for you, O my beloved.
   —Selections from The Song of Solomon (1–7) Holy Bible: New Revised
   Standard Version

8

I am not just a body for you
You have travelled further
Into me, with me, beyond yourself to me,
You have crossed boundaries
That encase me, enclose you,
Opened doors to new worlds,
Beneath new suns which know no settings,
Now you can cross oceans,
You will not leave me
A void like the silent shell on the shore.
You will be here in the rain
In the sunlight, walking, talking,
Laughing to the roofless skies,
You will be here in the sea,
In the storm, thinking, suffering, loving,
Merging in the million drops
Which know no bodies
No boundaries beyond this mystic mutuality

Where I am, where you are;
Now you can go to other bodies
Beyond this shore .
Love them, stir them,
Give them all of you and me
I can enchain them, encircle them,
Encompass them all
With your love and mine,
Desireless and free.
   —"I Am Not Just a Body for You" by Shakuntala Hawoldar (Mauritius)

I love you
because the Earth turns round the sun
because the North wind blows north
sometimes
because the Pope is Catholic
and most Rabbis Jewish
because winters flow into springs
and the air clears after a storm
because only my love for you
despite the charms of gravity
keeps me from falling off this Earth
into another dimension
I love you
because it is the natural order of things

I love you
like the habit I picked up in college
of sleeping through lectures
or saying I'm sorry
when I get stopped for speeding
because I drink a glass of water
in the morning
and chain-smoke cigarettes
all through the day
because I take my coffee Black
and my milk with chocolate
because you keep my feet warm
though my life a mess
I love you
because I don't want it
any other way

I am helpless
in my love for you
It makes me so happy
to hear you call my name
I am amazed you can resist
locking me in an echo chamber
where your voice reverberates
through the four walls
sending me into spasmatic ecstasy
I love you
because it's been so good
for so long
that if I didn't love you
I'd have to be born again
and that is not a theological statement
I am pitiful in my love for you

The Dells tell me Love
is so simple
the thought though of you
sends indescribably delicious multitudinous
thrills throughout and through-in my body
I love you
because no two snowflakes are alike
and it is possible
if you stand tippy-toe
to walk between the raindrops
I love you
because I am afraid of the dark
and can't sleep in the light
because I rub my eyes
when I wake up in the morning
and find you there
because you with all your magic powers were

determined that
I should love you
because there was nothing for you but that
I would love you
I love you
because you made me
want to love you
more than I love my privacy
my freedom my commitments
and responsibilities
I love you 'cause I changed my life
to love you
because you saw me one friday
afternoon and decided that I would
love you
I love you I love you I love you
    —"Resignation" by Nikki Giovanni

Once I asked for one lone petal of a rose,
To scent its fragrance, feel its touch.
And since I asked so little, I suppose,
I was given more than twice as much.

Once, in dreams, I asked one hour alone with you,
To sense your nearness, view your charms
As if my every wish had fallen due,
You spent the entire dream-night in my arms.
    —"The Compensation" by Ruth E. J. Sarver

@

When all my body has,
all my mind has
pounded out to press
symbols and seals into your waitingness—
WILL BE NOT ENOUGH!

Love's not enough to give you.
Any kiss
is not enough.
Any honey—sermons of the pulse that
I can confer, call forth
through eagle-hearts, through robins and vultures of giving,
through webs of thickened wanting in which are caught
Love-rack and rainbow—
WILL BE NOT ENOUGH!
   —"Love You Right Back" by Gwendolyn Brooks

I do not expect the spirit of Penelope
To enter my breast, for I am not mighty
Or fearless. (Only our love is brave,
A rock against the wind.) I cry and cringe
When the cyclops peer into my cave.

I do not expect your letters to be lengthy
And of love, flowery and philosophic, for
Words are not our bond.
I need only the hard fact
Of your existence for my subsistence.
Our love is a rock against the wind,
Not soft like silk and lace.
  —"A Love Poem" by Etheridge Knight

You are the gift of love to me
  —"Gift of Love" by Evelyn Maria Harris of Sweet Honey in the Rock

2

The voice of the wild goose shrills,
It is caught by its bait;
My love of you pervades me,
I cannot loosen it.
I shall retrieve my nets,
But what do I tell my mother,
To whom I go daily,
Laden with bird catch?
I have spread no snares today,
I am caught in my love of you!

3

The wild goose soars and swoops,
It alights on the net;
Many birds swarm about,
I have work to do.
I am held fast by my love,
Alone, my heart meets your heart,
From your beauty I'll not part!
—Ancient Egyptian Love Poems: Verses 2 and 3
from Papyrus Harris 500 IIb

I'm glad we drink from the same cup
Whether honey or whether brine,
I'll always drink my portion up
For your lot is cast with mine.

I'm glad we dance to the same song
Though the tune may vary some,

For we're still in step as we go along
Though you sing while I may hum.

As we travel along life's thoroughfare
Often uphill, stop and start,
We share a love so fine and rare
We're close even when we're apart.

I'll gladly share your joy and pain
If you cry, I'll dry your tears,
I'll stand by you in sun or rain
Through all of our earthbound years.

   —"Devoted to You" by Annette Jones White

You, my dear, are the sweet, the warm and beautiful—
Ever busy, ever conscious of your love and responsibility
to your family and friends.
God smiles and touches your face, ever so lightly,
Lifts the corners of your mouth, and hardened hearts melt.
He dips down into his bucket of sunshine and sprinkles
it all over you.
He massages your heart with his hands and brings it to
a burning flame of love for everyone—
You, You, You creature of God—You.

   —Dedication from *The Raw Pearl* by Pearl Bailey

Each
day with
you is like
the restful shade
a great oak tree gives.
You are cool meadows when
rain has fallen. You are my
constancy, my haven from storm.
　　—"For My Love" by Naomi Long Madgett

Testimonies of Love:
A Groom's Words For His Bride

You cheer my life with every smile.
—From *"Love's Morning Star"* by Marcus Garvey

W ell, after years of being a bachelor, you have finally found the love of your life. You have shredded your little black book, discarded those photos of your prior girlfriends, compared your fiancée's cooking to your mama's, and even stopped hanging with your homeboys on Saturday nights—all in the name of love.

You have never experienced such mystical feelings about a woman before. Every moment you spend with her you cherish. No other woman in the universe can make you feel the way your fiancée does. She is your sanctuary where you can seek shelter from the cold world. She intoxicates you with her passion, enthusiasm, worldliness, and beauty to the point where you become drunk with happiness. But yet she nourishes you as well with serenity, confidence, stability, and security—all in the name of love. She asks nothing of you but to be raptured through eternity in your love, fidelity, and friendship.

As the wedding day looms ever closer, such incredible feelings as these are probably going through your head. The selected readings in this section will help you translate some of these feelings into eloquent and powerful words. Why not express how your fiancée has

become such a vital part of you—almost as if you two have melded together as one—by reciting Frank Yerby's "You Are a Part of Me"? Or use one of these passages to make your wedding vows more special.

And
I will take you for my wife forever; I will take you for my wife in righteousness and in justice, in steadfast love, and in mercy. I will take you for my wife in faithfulness; and you shall know the Lord.

—Hosea (2:19–20) Holy Bible: New Revised Standard Version

My heart to thy heart,
    My hand to thine;
My lip to thy lips,
    Kisses are wine
Brewed for the lover in sunshine and shade;
Let me drink deep, then, my African maid.

Lily to lily,
    Rose unto rose;
My love to thy love
    Tenderly grows.

—From "Song" by Paul Laurence Dunbar

You are a part of me. I do not know
By what slow chemistry you first became
A vital fiber of my being. Go
Beyond the rim of time or space, the same
Inflections of your voice will sing their way
Into the depths of my mind still. Your hair
Will gleam as bright, the artless play
Of word and glance, gesture and the fair
Young fingers waving, have too deeply etched
The pattern of your soul on mine. Forget
Me quickly as a laughing picture sketched
On water, I shall never know regret
Knowing no magic ever can set free
That part of you that is a part of me.

   —"You Are a Part of Me" by Frank Yerby

Yours is not a beauty
To go unobserved
By others, nor myself,
But one to haunt

Our waking, sleeping, living,
And maybe our dying hours.
Yours is a beauty
Of dignity and of grace;
Yours is a beauty
Of line and of strength
Rivalled only by
The forest's richest ebony;
A beauty
Startlingly clothed in rose.

    —"Black Cameo on Pink Quartz" by John W. Burton

Her teeth are as white as the meat of an apple,
Her lips are like dark ripe plums.
I love her.
Her hair is a midnight mass, a dusky aurora.
I love her.
And because her skin is the brown of an oak leaf in autumn,
    but a softer color,
I want to kiss her.

    —"Fascination" by Langston Hughes

Love me Black Woman
Love me with the love
We lost on the hulking
Ships of slave merchants
Love me with the strength
Of the clanking chains
That tore flesh from
Our bone
Love me with all the
Black blood that watered
Fields of nations
Built upon our backs
Love me Black Woman
Love me
Love me with the hot rhythms
of our ancestral drums
The eternal fires of
Sacred black altars
Love me with the warm press
Of your thighs
And the soft swell of your belly
Filled with the children of our union
Love me Black Woman
Woman, woman, Oh Black Woman
Mother of the universe
Breeder of a million kings
Woman, Oh Black Woman
You who crawled with me
When I could not stand
Stood with me
When I could not walk
Lay with me

When I was unworthy
Woman, Oh Black Woman
Mother of all the shades
Of the rainbow
Love me, love me
Love me Black Woman
Love me now that I am worthy
Love me now that I am Man
Love me with the love that
Made me Man
The love that will make me a giant
The love that can make me a god
Love me Black Woman
Love me
Love me
Love me
   —"Love Me Black Woman" by Arnold Kemp

She is a friend of mind. She gather me, man. The pieces I am, she gather them and give them back to me in all the right order. It's good, you know, when you got a woman who is a friend of your mind.

   —From *Beloved* by Toni Morrison

Deep, deep is the root,
Deep in African soil;
Like sweet nectar of a fruit,
Long lean beauty still unspoiled.

Like enrapturing uncut gems,
completely free of piercing thorns;
grow your long, sturdy, uncut stems,
of which only an African sun adorns.

Appearing with a Zulu Maiden's pose,
new,
lovely,
black,
African beauty rose.
  —"African Beauty Rose" by Kattie M. Cumbo

Pale, delightful lady,
How I love you!
I would spread cool violets
At your feet
And bring you lovely jewels
For your hair,
And put a tiny golden ring
Upon your finger
And leave it there
As a sign and symbol of my love,
My bright, bright love for you.
Oh, pale, delightful lady,
How I love you!
  —"Pale Lady" by Langston Hughes

♥

Easter Sunday at twilight

Lenore,

With a heart that's full with a new found joy my thoughts turn
to you as the day closes, and a sigh rises as an evening prayer
to ask whatever gods there be to keep you safe for me. Since
first seeing you I have moved through the days as one in a
dream, lost in revery, awed by the speed with which the moving
finger of fate has pointed out the way I should go. As the miles
of countryside sped by on our return trip I sat silent and
pondered on the power that lies in a smile to change the course
of a life; the magic in the tilt of a head, the beauty of your
carriage and the gentleness that struck so deeply.

   Later, when I become more coherent, I shall say perhaps
many things but tonight this one thing alone seems to ring
clearly,

I love you.

Charlie
Washington, D.C.
April 9, 1939
   —A love letter from Charles R. Drew

O lady, be calm and cry not but sing to your suitors.

Sing to those who guide you and to the discerning passers-by.

Sing to the son of Shaka's people, cast aside your grief and
sorrow and distress.

O lady, be calm, let me give you gifts, fine clothes from our
homeland the Hejaz.

Let me adorn you with a chain and beads of gold devised in
Shiraz.

Let me build for you a great white house of lime and stone.

Let me furnish it for you with furnishings of crystal, so that
those who see it will be astonished by its construction,

Spread beneath with soft rushes from the lakesides of Shaka
and Ozi.

Let me satisfy your good parents and let them rest at ease with
minstrels' songs;

Let them lie at ease with food of the young of camels and of
many oxen, sheep and goats,

Because, my lady, O lady mine, let me tell you that you are my
beloved.

Let me tell you of my love so great that you may see it with
your own eyes.

Lift up your eyes and see, that everything may be plain to you.

Every good thing will I do for you, by the goodness of Almighty
God,

By his goodness and compassion that shines brightly like the
bright moonlight.

    —"Serenade" by an anonymous Kenyan author

You are but these to me: a freckled face,
Soft-lighted by a fragile smile, from lips

And eyes that shade a sorrow's ghost; a grace
As lightly balanced as a lark that dips
In restless pause before he seeks the stars;
A childyoung voice, that lullabies me peace,
Secure and warm, from life's diurnal wars
That fret the lonely mind without surcease.
You are remembered scent, imprinted on
A chair; a careless touch that burns within;
A glance that kisses from a table's length;
A subtle difference that you bring into
A room. But most, you are the woman
Who has taught me what it is to love.
    —"Sonnet Sequence I" by Darwin T. Turner

A capable wife who can find?
    She is far more precious than jewels.
The heart of her husband trusts in her,
    and he will have no lack of gain.
She does him good, and not harm,
    all the days of her life.
    —From Proverbs (31:10—12) Holy Bible: New Revised Standard Version

I could love her with a love so warm
You could not break it with a fairy charm;
I could love her with a love so bold
It would not die, e'en tho' the world grew cold.
  —Fenton Johnson

◆◆◆

Whilst tracing thy visage, I sink in emotion,
    For no other damsel so wond'rous I see;
Thy looks are so pleasing, thy charms so amazing,
    I think of no other, my true-love, but thee.

With heart-burning rapture I gaze on thy beauty,
    And fly like a bird to the boughs of a tree;
Thy looks are so pleasing, thy charms so amazing,
    I fancy no other, my true-love, but thee.

Thus oft in the valley I think and I wonder
    Why cannot a maid with her lover agree?
Thy looks are so pleasing, thy charms so amazing,
    I pine for no other, my true-love, but thee.

I'd fly from thy frowns with a heart full of sorrow—
    Return, pretty damsel, and smile thou on me;
By ev'ry endeavor, I'll try thee forever;
    And languish until I am fancied by thee.
  —"Love" by George Moses Horton

Nay, dearest, I will never thee forget,
  Who art so fair:
The flame still burns, 'tis not extinguished yet—
  Fond, sweetest dear.
  Methinks the changing scenes of life—
  In blissful peace or sullen strife—
Are not enough from mem'ry to efface
  Thy peerless grace.

What if by Fate's decree the path we tread—
  Of hapless crowds:
What though our heav'n of blue serene be spread
  With sombre clouds?
  'Twill be of this concern to me:
  A temple I'll erect to thee,
And always, dearest, sing thy praises there
  Softly,—and clear.

But ours is yet a blissful harmony:
  Could we but dream
Of things in future destined ours to be,
  Love were supreme.
  For thou art all heart can desire.
  Whate'er is pure thy grace inspire:
O loved one, thee—though we're asunder set—
  I'll ne'er forget.
  —"Forget Me Not" by J. B. Harlequin

How beautiful you are, my love,
    how very beautiful!
Your eyes are doves
    behind your veil.
Your hair is like a flock of goats,
    moving down the slopes of Gilead.
Your teeth are like a flock of shorn ewes
    that have come up from the washing,
all of which bear twins,
    and not one among them is bereaved.
Your lips are like a crimson thread,
    and your mouth is lovely.
Your cheeks are like halves of a pomegranate
    behind your veil.
Your neck is like the tower of David,
    built in courses;
on it hang a thousand bucklers,
    all of them shields of warriors.
Your two breasts are like two fawns,
    twins of a gazelle,
    that feed among the lilies.
Until the day breathes
    and the shadows flee,
I will hasten to the mountain of myrrh
    and the hill of frankincense.
You are altogether beautiful, my love;
    there is no flaw in you.
Come with me from Lebanon, my bride;
    come with me from Lebanon.
Depart from the peak of Amana,
    from the peak of Senir and Hermon,
from the dens of lions,

from the mountains of leopards.

You have ravished my heart, my sister, my bride,
  you have ravished my heart with a glance of your eyes,
  with one jewel of your necklace.
How sweet is your love, my sister, my bride!
  how much better is your love than wine,
  and the fragrance of your oils than any spice!
Your lips distill nectar, my bride;
  honey and milk are under your tongue;
  the scent of your garments is like the scent of Lebanon.
A garden locked is my sister, my bride,
  a garden locked, a fountain sealed.
Your channel is an orchard of pomegranates
  with all choicest fruits,
  henna with nard,
nard and saffron, calamus and cinnamon,
  with all trees of frankincense,
myrrh and aloes,
  with all chief spices—
a garden fountain, a well of living water,
  and flowing streams from Lebanon.
Awake, O north wind,
  and come, O south wind!
Blow upon my garden
  that its fragrance may be wafted abroad.
Let my beloved come to his garden,
  and eat its choicest fruits.

. . . .

How graceful are your feet in sandals,
  O queenly maiden!
Your rounded thighs are like jewels,
  the work of a master hand.
Your navel is a rounded bowl

that never lacks mixed wine.
Your belly is a heap of wheat,
    encircled with lilies.
Your two breasts are like two fawns,
    twins of a gazelle.
Your neck is like an ivory tower.
Your eyes are pools in Heshbon,
    by the gate of Bath-rabbim.
Your nose is like a tower of Lebanon,
    overlooking Damascus.
Your head crowns you like Carmel,
    and your flowing locks are like purple;
    a king is held captive in the tresses.

How fair and pleasant you are,
    O loved one, delectable maiden!
You are stately as a palm tree,
    and your breasts are like its clusters.
I say I will climb the palm tree
    and lay hold of its branches.
Oh, may your breasts be like clusters of the vine,
    and the scent of your breath like apples,
and your kisses like the best wine
    that goes down smoothly,
    gliding over lips and teeth.

. . . .

Set me as a seal upon your heart,
    as a seal upon your arm;
for love is strong as death,
    passion fierce as the grave.
Its flashes are flashes of fire,
    a raging flame.
Many waters cannot quench love,
    neither can floods drown it.

If one offered for love
　　all the wealth of his house,
　　it would be utterly scorned.
　　—Selections from The Song of Solomon (1–8) Holy Bible: New Revised
　　Standard Version

Come, take my hand, beloved, for it is midnight;
We have a rendezvous on a hillside with God.
He lives there and it will be easy to find Him.
The mantle of night will cover your hair;
Stars will serve as candle light;
I have fashioned you sandals for the meadows below;
On wings of night-wind we will hear soft singing;
The sea is a jewel afar and magnificent;
This night of our pilgrimage is beautiful;
It mirrors the serenity my soul finds in yours;
It holds heartbeats measuring our minutes together.
Hold fast my hand, beloved, we must go;
He waits there in the clover,
For I have made a promise
To come at midnight, in joyful thanksgiving,
For His gift of you to me.
　　—"Come, Beloved" by Will Smallwood

You are a child of
    The universe

A queen with great
    Beauty, poise and grace
Jewels and treasures
    Untold

Gentle quick smile
    Innocent eyes sparkling
Glowing like a wind-blown
    Candle in the dark

Ebony color skin
    Soft, warm, luster smooth
Sleek and sensuous

You are a child of
    The universe

From Africa to the
    Orient you travel
Lifetime after
    Lifetime
Conversing with gods, goddess
    Beings

Aristole, Socrates, Mai-Lo
    Kant, Shaka-Zulu
Cleopathra

You are my ebony
    Woman
Flowing through the
Wind

Dancing with the
   Night
   —"Universal Woman" by Tommye Lee Ray

I love to see the big white moon,
   A-shining in the sky;
I love to see the little stars,
   When the shadow clouds go by.

I love the rain drops falling
   On my roof-top in the night;

I love the soft wind's sighing,
   Before the dawn's gray light.

I love the deepness of the blue,
   In my Lord's heaven above;
But better than all these things I think,
   I love my lady love.
   —"My Loves" by Langston Hughes

It was only a dream,
Or so it seemed!
Because we all know,
That love doesn't happen at first sight.
At least not in real life!
Maybe in fairy tales,
And mystical myths
Of fantasy lands
In places far far away
And ages long time gone.
But not for real!
Yet there was that warm,
Dying winter's night
When the dawning of Spring
Was just beyond the horizon,
And the fragrance of freshly bloomed gardenias
Caressed the evening sky.
And I,
Regal and Proud,
Aglow in all my Royal Majesty,
Sailed into the smoke-filled room
That was tinged with the scent
Of freshly harvested herb
And the melodic rhythms
Of Mother Terra's
Most ancient and advanced tribes.
Only to meet
She, for whom my soul has
Eternally longed to greet.
We glanced,
And in that look
All of time ceased,

Eternity unveiled before our eyes,
And we knew that we had always been one!
　—"Wings of the Phoenix" by Nirvana Reginald Gayle

Over the seas tonight, love,
　Over the darksome deeps,
Over the seas tonight, love,
　Slowly my vessel creeps.

Over the seas tonight, love,
　Walking the sleeping foam—
Sailing away from thee, love,
　Sailing from thee and home.

Over the seas tonight, love,
　Dreaming beneath the spars—
Till in my dreams you shine, love,
　Bright as the listening stars.
　—"Sea Lyric" by William Stanley Braithwaite

I wanna be somebody
fragrant
in your life
wanna cloud you with my scents

overcast as pine
overcast as pine

I wanna be a
bouquet
in your mouth
wanna flavor you
with my mists

flowers like honeysuckle
flowers like honeysuckle

I wanna bloom in your fingerprints
sprout a weak willingness
entangle your grinning heart
till it blossoms & pumps sweet fertilizer
into our unending high country

perfume rises from our breathless footsteps
your sugar ripens my touch
my syrup honeys your skin

I wanna float in your memories
melt on your horizon
I wanna be somebody
fragrant
in your time
wanna wisp of me to defy dilution

dew can't

storm can't

I wanna be invisible
so I can seep into the back door of your pores
　—"Be Somebody Fragrant" by Peter J. Harris

Why should I sing when every living voice
　　Carols in joy for my love's holiday?
Why should I laugh when all the skies rejoice,
　　Blue-girt and silvered in each sun-kissed ray?
Yea, though the skies, the earth, each God-sent thing,
　　In flowering field, or glen, or deep-set moor,
Croon softly each to each, still shall I sing,
　　Tho weak the chords or be the accents poor.
These shall I bring for my love's golden fare,
　　These shall I give as down my days she trips—
Song-burthened zephyrs for her wind-blown hair,
　　Garlands of laughter for her crimson lips,
Laughter or song, 'tis but love's joyous fee,
Deep from the treasure of my heart to thee.
　—"IV" by Joseph S. Cotter Jr.

"I'm grateful to *you*, Stella. I mean you are the one person I can actually talk to about anything and you don't bite your tongue and I don't have to pretend to be something that I'm not with you and you make me feel really good about being who I am. And you make me laugh. Not very many people, girls, women, can make me laugh."

—From *How Stella Got Her Groove Back* by Terry McMillan

I dreamed that I was a rose
That grew beside a lonely way,
Close by a path none ever chose,
And there I lingered day by day.
Beneath the sunshine and the show'r
I grew and waited there apart,
Gathering perfume hour by hour,
And storing it within my heart,
    Yet, never knew,
Just why I waited there and grew.

I dreamed that you were a bee
That one day gaily flew along,
You came across the hedge to me,
And sang a soft, love-burdened song.
You brushed my petals with a kiss,
I woke to gladness with a start,
And yielded up to you in bliss
The treasured fragrance of my heart;
    And then I knew
That I had waited there for you.

    —"The Awakening" by James Weldon Johnson

OUR LOVE

Our love is a rock against the wind
—From "A Love Poem" by Etheridge Knight

T he collection of readings assembled in "Our Love" allows the bride and groom to share with their wedding guests a private glimpse of their love for each other. It is your way to show just how special and unique the love between the two of you truly is. The readings in "Our Love" should be read aloud by the bride and groom, or a reader, for all wedding guests to rejoice in.

Gordon Parks's spirited verse showcases the love Gordon has for his wife—a timeless love with no beginning nor end in sight. Naomi Long Madgett's "Wedding Song" acknowledges that love between two people changes, often moving beyond romantic love to a seasoned love that becomes more intense and all-consuming with the passage of time. And Fenton Johnson eloquently compares love to the power of a God—without the passion of love there would be no sun or moon for us to see the beauty that nature provides.

Beloved, let us love one another, because love is from God; everyone who loves is born of God and knows God. Whoever does not love does not know God, for God is love. God's love was revealed among us in this way: God sent his only Son into the world so that we might live through him. In this is love, not that we loved God but that he loved us and sent his Son to be the atoning sacrifice for our sins. Beloved, since God loved us so much, we also ought to love one another. No one has ever seen God; if we love one another, God lives in us, and his love is perfected in us.

—John (4:7–12) Holy Bible: New Revised Standard Version

I came to the crowd seeking friends
I came to the crowd seeking love
I came to the crowd for understanding

I found you

I came to the crowd to weep
I came to the crowd to laugh

You dried my tears
You shared my happiness

I went from the crowd seeking you
I went from the crowd seeking me
I went from the crowd forever

You came, too
    —"You Came, Too" by Nikki Giovanni

HE: My love for you is strong,
    Like the oak tree grows.
    My love for you is full
    Like a sun-kissed rose.

SHE: My love for you is real,
    Like day after night.
    My love for you is warm,
    Like morning sunlight.

HE: My love for you is pure,
    Like water from a spring.
    My love for you is free,
    Like eagles on the wing.

SHE: My love for you is soft,
    Like the west wind's sigh.
    My love for you is deep,
    Like a midnight sky.

HE: My love for you is sweet,
    Like the "gods' " own wine.

SHE: My love for you is hungry,
    Come and let me dine.
    —"Lovers' Dialogue" by Annette Jones White

All yesterday it poured, and all night long
    I could not sleep; the rain unceasing beat
Upon the shingled roof like a weird song,
    Upon the grass like running children's feet.
And down the mountains by the dark cloud kissed,
    Like a strange shape in filmy veiling dressed,
Slid slowly, silently, the wraith-like mist,
    And nestled soft against the earth's wet breast.

But lo, there was a miracle at dawn!
    The still air stirred at touch of the faint breeze,
The sun a sheet of gold bequeathed the lawn,
    The songsters twittered in the rustling trees.
And all things were transfigured in the day,
    But me whom radiant beauty could not move;
For you, more wonderful, were far away,
    And I was blind with hunger for your love.
    —"Summer Morn in New Hampshire" by Claude McKay

Dream about me.
Call me darling.
Whisper loving words, my dear,
How you always will adore me.
That is what I want to hear.
Breathe the thought
That naught can part us,
And forever you'll be true.
Then remember, oh, my darling,
My heart and thoughts are all for you.

Make your plans
So they'll include me
In your life from this day on.
I could never be content
If your love was past and gone.
Life grows sweeter
When the living
Is with one who holds you dear,
And your love shall be my fortress
Even when cold death is near.

If you should leave
This world before me
For a mansion in the sky,
Tell the keeper of the portal
To wait; my soul will soon be nigh.
Go, not too far, into Heaven
Where the loved ones part no more.
Wait, my darling, wait for me
Just inside of Heaven's door.
  —"Dream about Me" by Nathaniel I. Twitt

It was on the top of a hill beneath
The glittering stars that I saw you—
A hill shaped like the vaulted sky
Of heaven, and all strange and new.
From below was heard the gentle ripple
Of a flowing stream, and O, how I
Was enchanted by its distant song—
And by you, and the stars, and the sky.
How I long to catch the spirit
Of that night, and hold it fast, then draw
Upon my canvas, eternal and divine,
That moment so filled with love and awe!
    —"Enchantment" by Georgia Holloway Jones

♦♦♦

Moving deep
more and
more
in me

the thought
    of you
        comes and comes

in me
this joy,
the thought
of you.
    —"Moving Deep" by Stephany

we can be anything we want
for we are the young ones
walken without footprints
moven our bodies in tune
to songs
      echoen us. the beautiful
black ones.
      recently born.
           walken new
           rhythms
leaven behind us a tap dancer's dream
of sunday nite ed sullivan shows.
WE WILL BE
      ALL that we want
for we are the young ones
bringen the world to a Black Beginnen.
  —"We Can Be" by Sonia Sanchez

Your hands in my hands,
  Happily meet;
Your eyes and my eyes,
  Joyously greet;
Your cheek 'gainst my cheek,
  Passingly sweet;
Your lips to my lips,
  Rapture complete.
  —"Poem #63" by Joseph S. Cotter Jr.

Before I took my mother's blood and breath
        I loved you.
When you broke the silence of your first hour
        crying
Through ovaled eyes under some foreign sky,
I had already begun to guard your days.
        Each moonfall after,
I tossed a lotus petal into my river of hopes
Until an endless bouquet covered the oceans
        that parted us.
Through winter-locked and hungered days,
        in
The trials of many doubtful years, and over
Hourless and mistaken roads I searched for you.
If, as you say, during pillow talk, you do not know me,
        It is because I am you.
I have been you for a thousand years.
Our love is older than the air.

    —From a letter written by Gordon Parks to his wife, from *Voices in the Mirror*

Without the passion love, no sun would glow,
No golden moon would grace the summer eve;
The golden-rod would cease to charm the eye;
The gilded rose would wither ere its day,
And all the general universe be black;
For when within thy heart thou know'st that Love
Hath wrought his miracle, thou art a God,
And all that is of earth is slave to thee.

    —From "The Lover's Soliloquy" by Fenton Johnson

70

Ruth said:

"Do not press me to leave you
    or to turn back from following you!
Where you go, I will go;
    Where you lodge, I will lodge;
your people shall be my people,
    and your God my God.
Where you die, I will die—
    there will I be buried.
May the Lord do thus and so to me,
    and more as well,
if even death parts me from you!"
    —Ruth (1:16–17) Holy Bible: New Revised Standard Version

Leona and Jesse were escaped slaves on the run in Wynton Marsalis's Pulitzer Prize—winning jazz oratorio. In their song "I Hold Out My Hand," Leona offers her love to soothe Jesse's pain. In their journey they discovered their love conquered anguish, their love captured soul.

*What has more meaning than pain? He wants to know
    what soul is?*
Leona: I hold out my hand
            To comfort your wounds
            And give without want
            The sweetness of life.
            Through rivers of tears
            The moon shines tonight.
            And that is what soul is.
            When this bitter life has ended

Death may be a welcome rest
But why waste all your living on dying?
Why let mocking evil spirits have their way?
Why wallow in sorrow
When love's joys can be found?
Oh, come to me until I feel your heartbeat
And when our hearts are swaying at one tempo
That is soul.

Jesse: I have no heart, it's been crushed and torn by misery.
What sweet softness, can a man know in his heart
When others buy and sell his loved ones?
Is that soul?
And when this bitter life has ended
I will dance a happy dance
I will sing
I will shout
I will cry
And in my rage I will—O why!
Anguished heart! Wake my ears to hear this
woman's song
Soul is the giving without want.
The sharing of some soothing sweetness through this
bitter life.

Leona: Come to me until I feel your heartbeat
When our hearts are swaying at one tempo

Jesse: Yes, I think I understand what soul is.

Leona: Come and let us have this dance

Jesse: Come and let us have this dance
That is soul.

Leona and Jesse:
My lips are sweet
(just one little taste)
My bosom not cold
(just one little taste)

Let's pleasure ourselves
(just one little taste)
Romance can't be sold
(but they sure will try)
But even through tears
(and there are many)
The moon shines tonight
(let's stop this talking)
And that is what soul is!

—"I Hold Out My Hand" from *Blood on the Fields* by Wynton Marsalis

I cannot swear with any certainty
That I will always feel as I do now,
Loving you with the same fierce ecstasy,
Needing the same your lips upon my brow.
Nor can I promise stars forever bright
Or vow green leaves will never turn to gold.
I cannot see beyond this present night
To say what promises the dawn may hold.
And yet I know my heart must follow you
High up to hilltops, low through vales of tears,
Through golden days and days of somber hue.
And love will only deepen with the years
Becoming sun and shadow, wind and rain,
Wine that grows mellow, bread that will sustain.

—"Wedding Song" by Naomi Long Madgett

BLESSINGS FOR THE BRIDE AND GROOM

Let your love be like the misty rains, coming
softly, but flooding the river.

—*A Madagascar saying*

*M*any of your closest friends and relatives may want to participate in the celebration of your blessed wedding day beyond
just being a wedding guest. One of the greatest honors bestowed
upon a friend or relative is to ask him or her to read a blessing to you
and your partner during the wedding ceremony. Imagine a child just
learning to read giving their first public recital with a few words from
one of the short quotes. Imagine the groom's best friend—Mr. Bachelor—reading about love and fidelity.

The following collection of "Blessings" may also inspire your
reader to write original blessings or simply recite from the collection.
The blessings have been gathered from all over the African diaspora
so you should find a reading that captures the essence of the blessings that you desire.

Given that many of these blessings are in the form of a prayer, you
may want to touch base with the clergy officiating at your wedding to
ensure that he or she has not selected similar blessings.

Then I heard what seemed to be the voice of a great multitude,
like the sound of many waters and like the sound of mighty
thunderpeals, crying out,
"Hallelujah!
For the Lord our God
the Almighty reigns.
Let us rejoice and exult
and give him the glory,
for the marriage of the Lamb has come,
and his bride has made herself ready;
to her it has been granted to be clothed
with fine linen, bright and pure"—
for the fine linen is the righteous deeds of the saints.
—Revelations (19:6—8) Holy Bible: New Revised Standard Version

Receive this holy fire.
Make your lives like this fire.
A holy life that is seen.
A life of God that is seen.
A life that has no end.
A life that darkness does not overcome.
May this light of God in you grow.
Light a fire that is worthy of your heads.
Light a fire that is worthy of your children.
Light a fire that is worthy of your fathers.
Light a fire that is worthy of your mothers.
Light a fire that is worthy of God.
Now go in peace.
May the Almighty protect you
today and all days.

   —"Light a Holy Fire" is a prayer from the Masai in Tanzania

I just wanted you to know that you fill my life (and the lives of so many of those around you) with joy, with love, with the promise of dreams fulfilled.

I am elated, inspired, curious, expectant—just plain thrilled—by you, by your love, by your friendship, by the thought of our moving through life in some sort of synchronized tandem.

I'll be loving you always—and admiring you just as long.

I call the world to come and see!

—A letter by the late Melissa Carleton Pearson written to her friend Kimberly Hatchett-Maitland in celebration of Kim's wedding, dated April 26, 1991.

Libations! Libations!
To the protective spirits on high!
To the wandering spirits below!
To the spirits of the mountains,
To the spirits of the valleys,
To the spirits of the East,
To the spirits of the West,
To the spirits of the North,
To the spirits of the South,
To the bride and groom, together, libation!
May the spirits on high, as well as the spirits below, fill you with
    grace!
Divine helpers, come! Keep watch all night! Rather than see the
    bridegroom so much as damage his toenail, may the good
    spirits go ahead of him. May the bride not so much as
    damage her fingernail! The good spirits will be their cushions
    so that not a hair of their heads shall be harmed.

    And you, all you good wedding guests waiting in the
    shadows, come out into the light! May the light follow you!
—Anonymous African wedding benediction

By warm blood of bird
By wing of bird
By feather of bird
Let our love be safe.

By hot blood of mammal
By fur and by hair
By mammary gland
Let it come to no harm.

By chill blood of reptile
By scale of reptile
By lung of reptile
Let no ill damage it.

By four-legged amphibian
By gill and naked skin
By slow blood and lung
Adapt and be nourished.

By cool blood of fish
By gill and by fin
By scale and skeleton
Let no harm come to our love.
　　—"Spell to Protect Our Love" by Jeni Couzyn

To-day is
not Saturday
today is
not just another day
today is
Creation day
man and woman
becoming
one
   East and West
   have come together
   North and South, depths and heights
   witness this
   birth
To-day is
not just another day
to-day is
Celebration day
Communion day
   drumming and dancing
   singing and feasting
   blessing this
   birth
Yet drumming must cease
calling an end to our dance
the song of feasting
must break
into rhythms
of an every day
to-day will be
to-day
to-morrow is

family day
My age-mate
we must leave
taking with us
the melodies of
this day
for ever
humming in our ears
for to-day is
not just another day
Our bride and groom
my life
your life, our life
family life
for ever bubble
vibrate
with to-day's joyful echoes
blessing
this birth, our birth . . .
  Come friends
  come all
  come join hands
  come and witness.
  —"At an Age-Mate's Wedding" by Mícere M.G. Mūgo

Find the soul . . .
Never mind words or gestures.
Flowers and dinners are nice.
Sweetness, a Kiss, perfume
    and summer walks, timely.

Two sets of eyes
Tracking the moon,
But, find the soul . . .
And wait there forever.
Never leave,
No matter how long
They stay away—wandering,

Searching outside themselves.

Wait in the soul
Until you hear them crawling,
Running or being chased back . . .

Then, open their souls to them.
Open them to themselves
By the you in them.

Show them how the longest trip
Begins and ends in a footstep.
Find the soul . . .
Never mind
Words or gestures, Lovers.
    —"To Lovers" by Richard W. Thomas

May God agree with us.
Yes, my God, you will save us:
yes, my God, you will guide us,
and your thoughts will be with us night and day.
Grant us to remain a long time,
like the great wing of rain, like the long rains.
Give us the fragrance of a purifying branch.
Be the support of our burdens,
and may they always be untied,
the shells of fertility and mothers and children.
God be our safeguard, also where the shepherds are.
God, sky, with stars at your sides
and the moon in the middle of your stomach,
morning of my God that is rising,
come and hit us with your waters.
And God said: "All right."

    —A prayer from the Samburu in Kenya

Almighty God, our heavenly Father, the privilege is
ours to share in the loving, healing, reconciling mission of
your Son Jesus Christ, our Lord, in this age and wherever we
are. Since without you we can do no good thing.
     May your Spirit make us wise;
     May your Spirit guide us;
     May your Spirit renew us;
     May your Spirit strengthen us;
So that we will be:
Strong in faith,
Discerning in proclamation,
Courageous in witness,
Persistent in good deeds.
This we ask through the name of the Father.
     —Prayer from the Church of the Province of the West Indies

All shall be Amen and Alleluia.
We shall rest and we shall see,
We shall see and we shall know.
We shall know and we shall love.
We shall love and we shall praise.
Behold our end which is no end.
     —"Amen and Alleluia" by Saint Augustine

Not with my hands
But with my heart I bless you:
May peace forever dwell
Within your breast!

May Truth's white light
Move with you and possess you—
And may your thoughts and words
Wear her bright crest!

May Time move down
Its endless path of beauty
Conscious of you
And better for your being!

Spring after Spring
Array itself in splendor

Seeking the favor
Of your sentient seeing!

May hills lean toward you,
Hills and windswept mountains,
And trees be happy
That have seen you pass—

Your eyes dark kinsmen
To the stars above you—
Your feet remembered
By the blades of grass . . . !
    —"Benediction" by Donald Jeffrey Hayes

Why should there have been so much of pomp and ceremony—flowers and carriages and silk hats; wedding cake and wedding music? After all marriage in its essence is and should be very simple: a clasp of a friendly hand; a walking away together of Two who say: "Let us try to be One and face and fight a lonely world together!" What more? Is that not enough?

 —From "So the Girl Marries" by W. E. B. Du Bois, written for the wedding of Yolande Du Bois and Countee Cullen

Lord of the springtime, Father of flower, field and fruit, smile on us in these earnest days when the work is heavy and the toil wearisome; lift up our hearts, O God, to the things worthwhile— sunshine and night, the dripping rain, the song of the birds, books and music, and the voices of our friends. Lift up our hearts to these this night, O Father, and grant us Thy peace. Amen.

 —Prayer by W. E. B. Du Bois

The Lord make us mindful of the little things that grow and blossom in these days to make the world beautiful for us. Teach us to reverence in this world not simply the great and impressive but all the minute and myriad-sided beauty of field and flower and tree. And as we worship these, so in our lives let us strive not for the masterful and spectacular but for the good and true, not for the thunder but for the still small voice of duty.
Amen.

 —Prayer by W. E. B. Du Bois

Heavenly father, hear us as we pray here at this your altar on their wedding day. Show them the path you would have them take, help them to follow thee and sin forsake. In their heart oh God this day they have come to pledge their love and unity blessed by sacred vows. Make and keep them one through all eternity. Give them strength, your strength in sorrow want or pain help them steadfast to remain. Whenever clouds should fill their skies of blue, Lord help their love and your grace shall see them through. Father until they reach life's ebbing tide may they in perfect love and peace abide. You have promised never to leave us nor forsake us, we claim that promise in this union, in their love and life together. And when life's sun shall set one day beyond a hill, it is our prayer that they will still be hand in hand. For we ask it in the name of Jesus Christ our Lord. Let the church say Amen.

—From the vows of Rita and Jawanza Kunjufu provided by Reverend Jeremiah A. Wright Jr.

My best friend . . .

is a high-siddity,
   sophisticated,
      grown-up woman,
         hiding skateboard-skidded knees
            under her fashionable skirts.

I know because I was there.

Your mom's mac & cheese
   My mom's curry chicken.
      Church at the Johnson's
         Upsouth in Queens, New York.
            My double-dutching,
               doll-playing,
                  ice skating,
                     kango-krewin' bloodsister.

I was there.

God sent you a gift in this man you have become part of,
   adding an "s" to the friend in my best . . .

Noah's pair,
   teaching me, giving me no choice
      but to believe in love again
         as the evidence stands before me.

(Sherwin, here's a secret, I was always rooting for you.)

My sister and brother, your beautiful black love beckons
   sunshine . . .

Ginger, I am honored to give you to your new best friend.
   —Poem by Abiola Abrams, read at the wedding of Ginger Crenshaw
   and Sherwin Brown

You shall no more be termed Forsaken,
    and your land shall no more be termed Desolate;
but you shall be called My Delight Is in Her,
    and your land Married;
for the Lord delights in you,
    and your land shall be married.
For as a young man marries a young woman,
    so shall your builder marry you,
and as the bridegroom rejoices over the bride,
    so shall your God rejoice over you.
    —Isaiah (62:4—5) Holy Bible: New Revised Standard Version

Your world is as big as you make it.
I know, for I used to abide
In the narrowest nest in a corner,
My wings pressing close to my side.

But I sighted the distant horizon
Where the sky line encircled the sea
And I throbbed with a burning desire
To travel this immensity.

I battered the cordons around me
And cradled my wings on the breeze
Then soared to the uttermost reaches
With rapture, with power, with ease!
    —"Your World" by Georgia Douglas Johnson

"But
from the beginning of creation, 'God made them male and
female.' 'For this reason a man shall leave his father and mother
and be joined to his wife, and the two shall become one flesh.'
So they are no longer two, but one flesh. Therefore what God
has joined together, let no one separate."
  —Mark (10:6—9) Holy Bible: New Revised Standard Version

I

This love is a rich cry over
the deviltries and death
A weapon-song. Keep it strong.

Keep it strong.
Keep it logic and Magic and lightning and Muscle.

Strong hand in strong hand, stride to
the Assault that is promised you (knowing
no armor assaults a pudding or a mush.)

Here is your Wedding Day.
Here is your launch.

Come to your Wedding Song.

II

For you
I wish the kindness that romps or sorrows along.
Or kneels.
I wish you the daily forgiveness of each other.
For war comes in from the World

and puzzles a darling duet—
tangles tongues,
tears hearts, mashes minds;
there will be the need to forgive.

I wish you the jewels of black love.

Come to your Wedding Song.
  —"A Black Wedding Song" by Gwendolyn Brooks

Dark an' stormy may come de wedder;
I jines dis he-male an' dis she-male togedder.
Let none, but Him dat makes de thunder,
Put dis he-male an' dis she-male asunder.
I darefor 'nounce you bofe de same.
Be good, go 'long, an' keep up yo' name.
De broomstick's jumped, de world's not wide.
She's now yo' own. Salute yo' bride!
  —A Slave Marriage Ceremony

I dream a world where man
No other man will scorn,
Where love will bless the earth
And peace its paths adorn.
I dream a world where all
Will know sweet freedom's way,
Where greed no longer saps the soul
Nor avarice blights our day.
A world I dream where black or white,
Whatever race you be,
Will share the bounties of the earth
And every man is free,
Where wretchedness will hang its head
And joy, like a pearl,
Attends the needs of all mankind—
Of such I dream, my world!
   —"I Dream a World" by Langston Hughes

Making Our Love Fun

In fact, through all the years of my marriage, my love for Camille, like my stomach, has steadily grown.

—From *Love and Marriage* by Bill Cosby

*L*aughter is one of the key ingredients in the recipe for a successful marriage. No matter what you cook up in your marriage, you must always sprinkle your concoction with some TLC and laughter.

So as you plan your wedding day laugh a little. Enjoy the planning process no matter how insurmountable some of the problems may seem—a few years from now you will have a good chuckle as you remember the many hours you spent deciding on what shade of white linen napkins you should place on your wedding register. On your wedding day you can look back in bliss knowing that most people will not really notice the shade of cream of the wedding dress, the tails or lack of tails on the groomsmen's tuxedos, the missing baby's breath in the centerpieces, or the choice of four hors d'oeuvres instead of five.

To shed a little laughter and humor on your forthcoming nuptials, read through the following pages and have a laugh courtesy of me. Remember to read some of these writings aloud to add a little spice to your bridal shower or bachelor party!

He who finds a wife finds a good thing, and obtains favor from the Lord.
—Proverbs (18:22) Holy Bible: New Revised Standard Version

Untouched by the plow,
Free of the grain,
Innocent of the sweat of man or beast,
Bathed only in the waters of the rain,
Warmed by the sun time and time again,
Painted by the moon that shines from beyond—
You are virgin now—
But for how long?
—"Virgin Field" by Arthur Braziel

Love is like a virus. It can happen to anybody at any time.
—Maya Angelou

Nay, do not blush! I only heard
  You had a mind to marry;
I thought I'd speak a friendly word,
  So just one moment tarry.

Wed not a man whose merit lies
  In things of outward show,
In raven hair or flashing eyes,
  That please your fancy so.

But marry one who's good and kind,
  And free from all pretence;
Who, if without a gifted mind,
  At least has common sense.
  —"Advice to the Girls" by Francis Ellen Watkins Harper

Often a man's mother has difficulty getting along with the woman her son marries. This is especially true if the man involved expects the two women to be rivals and, secretly or otherwise, enjoys seeing them fight over him.
  —From *We Flew over the Bridge* by Faith Ringgold

You must pay the price
Of wanting to marry
A university graduate,
A Ph.D. at that!
She's worth every bit
Of six thousand naira;
We must uphold tradition.

Agreed, but then
Can you give a guarantee
She's not shop-soiled—
All those years on the campus,
Swotting and sweating,
Sucking up to lecturers
For all those degrees?

Shop-soiled, you ask?
What do you mean 'shop-soiled'?
Our daughter's not old clothes,
She's not old books
That get soiled in the shop;
She's old wine, matured over the years
For the discerning taste.

Shop-soiled she may not be,

Matured no doubt she is;
But then is she untouched?
Has nobody removed the cork,
All those years in the varsity?

That we cannot tell you,
That's your business to find out
On your nuptial night
In the privacy of your bedroom.

In that case, in-laws, dear,
Can I return her then
And obtain a refund
According to tradition
If I should discover
Someone has sipped the wine
Before I got there?
    —"Bride Price" by Mabel Segun (Nigeria)

All you need in the world is love and laughter. That's all anybody needs. To have love in one hand and laughter in the other.
    —August Wilson

I heard it said that I was betrothed
And one afternoon when I was at home,
As I was sitting, I saw a fool coming.
He came dragging his coat on the ground
And his trousers were made of khaki.
I said to him, 'Fool, where do you come from?'
He replied, 'I am your betrothed.'
I gave the dog a chair and his tail hung down.
    —"I Am Your Betrothed" by anonymous (Botswana)

I

You have reached the place of weariness,
You have arrived and you will get weary!
You have left your father's house,
You have deserted the hut of your mother.

II

You will need a rope to tether him!
I-yo-i tɔhi-tɔhi-tɔhi!
You will have to tie him up!
If you want to call him husband
You will have to tie him up!

III

Hey, young bride!
Yes?
Let's go and draw water.
I'm not going, I'm ill.
Hey, young bride! You're wanted in the bridal chamber!
    Lazy little lump goes toddling off!
    Little bandy-legs goes toddling off!

Hey, young bride!
Yes?
Let's go and cultivate.
I'm not going, I'm ill.
Hey, young bride! You're wanted in the bridal chamber!
    Lazy little lump goes toddling off!
    Little bandy-legs goes toddling off!
    —"The Bride's Arrival" by anonymous (Zulu)

Mandy Johnson wears a smile—
What makes Mandy pleased the while?
There are rumors in the town—
Mandy has a weddin' gown.

The stripes are big, and the stripes are red
And there is a hood to fit the head:
And they say no queen or crown
Ever was like Mandy's gown.

There were laces there were beads—
There were velvets there were seeds:
And from the girdle hanging down
Was a blue ribbon on the gown.

Mandy learned to stitch and sew—
To make that gown to please her beau:
And he declared did Mistah Brown
There never was such a weddin' gown.

Before the parson Mandy stands
Holding her honey's horny hands,
And their blushes soft and brown
Were spread all over that weddin' gown.

There was a party and a dance—
And soft the whispering and the glance.
And the song that most went round
Was glory, glory, to that gown.
    —"The Weddin' Gown," an anonymous plantation poem

His snores
protect the sleeping hut
but the day's
load
and the morrow's
burden
weigh heavily over
the stooping mother as she
sweeps the hut
bolts the pen
tidies the hearth
buries the red charcoals
and finally seeks
her restless bed

His snores
welcome her to bed
four hours to sunrise
His snores rouse her from bed
six sharp
Arise
O, wife of the husband!
  —"Wife of the Husband" by Mícere M.G. Mũgo

If you want to live long with your wife—you must be patient.
  —An African proverb

Oh beautiful bride, don't cry,
Your marriage will be happy.
Console yourself, your husband will be good.
And like your mother and your aunt,
You will have many children in your life:
Two children, three children, four . . .

Resign yourself, do like all others.
A man is not a leopard,
A husband is not a thunder-stroke,
Your mother was your father's wife;
It will not kill you to work.

It will not kill you to grind the grain,
Nor will it kill you to wash the pots.
Nobody dies from gathering firewood
Nor from washing clothes.

We did not do it to you,
We did not want to see you go;
We love you too much for that.
It's your beauty that did it,
Because you are so gorgeous . . .
Ah, we see you laugh beneath your tears!

Goodbye, your husband is here
And already you don't seem
To need our consolations . . .
   —"Song of the Bridesmaids" by Rwanda (Rwanda)

Oh, I am gone,
Oh, I am gone,
Call my father that I may say farewell to him,
Oh, I am gone.
Father has already sold me,

Mother has received a high price for me,
Oh, I am gone.
    —"Bride's Farewell Song" by Baganda (Uganda)

Yes, let us now set forth one of the fundamental truths about marriage: the wife is in charge. Or, to put it another way, the husband is not. Now I can hear your voices crying out:

What patronizing nonsense.
What a dumb generalization.

What a great jacket for the Salvation Army.

Well, my proof of the point is a simple one. If any man truly believes that he is the boss of his house, then let him do this: pick up the phone, call a wallpaper store, order new wallpaper for one of the rooms in his house, and then put it on. He would have a longer life expectancy sprinkling arsenic on his eggs. Any husband who buys wallpaper, drapes, or even a prayer rug on his own is auditioning for the Bureau of Missing Persons.

Therefore, in spite of what Thomas Jefferson wrote, all men may be created equal, but not to all women, and the loveliest love affair must bear the strain of this inequality once the ceremony is over. When a husband and wife settle down together, there is a natural struggle for power (I wonder why he bothers);

and in this struggle, the husband cannot avoid giving up a few things—for example, dinner.

—From *Love and Marriage* by Bill Cosby

A Wedding Gift: Words of Wisdom for the Bride and Groom

There is no secret to a long marriage—it's hard work. . . . It's serious business, and certainly not for cowards.

—*Ossie Davis*

To make this book even more special for you, here is a wedding gift to you. This section of passages provides words of advice to the bride and groom through poetry and prose. Like a plant, a marriage needs nurturing. A beautiful wedding ceremony does not guarantee a successful marriage, but rather the time and energy a couple puts into a marriage will blossom into an eternal relationship that will weather the test of time. If a husband and wife take each other for granted, a marriage is sure to wither from a lack of nurturing.

Mutual respect, trust, support, selflessness, commitment, love, and friendship are needed to make any marriage grow strong through the years. Without these core tenets, a marriage is destined to fail. Marriage is a symbiotic relationship—as the years evaporate you grow increasingly dependent on each other. Each of you receives sustenance from being together, almost as if you are joined at the hip. As the Bible (Ephesians 5:31) states: "A man will leave his father and mother and be joined to his wife, and the two will become one flesh."

Perhaps for your wedding ceremony, you might ask couples whose marriages you admire to share their words of wisdom for a successful marriage through an original reading or one from this section. You could also ask the officiant at your wedding to read a passage from this chapter.

Be subject to one another out of reverence for Christ. . . . Husbands, love your wives, just as Christ loved the church and gave himself up for her, in order to make her holy by cleansing her with the washing of water by the word, so as to present the church to himself in splendor, without a spot or wrinkle or anything of the kind—yes, so that she may be holy and without blemish. In the same way, husbands should love their wives as they do their own bodies. He who loves his wife loves himself. For no one ever hates his own body, but he nourishes and tenderly cares for it, just as Christ does for the church, because we are members of his body. "For this reason a man will leave his father and mother and be joined to his wife, and the two will become one flesh."

—Ephesians (5:21,25–31) Holy Bible: New Revised Standard Version

Romantic love flourishes with mutual respect, which, in turn, is engendered by a commitment by both to nourish the relationship and each other. Yes, duty plays a part in love, as unromantic as that may sound, but it is a duty that is lovingly and cheerfully borne.

There may be times when, by necessity, one partner takes charge of a specific aspect of the relationship, but the contributions of each should balance out over time. We need to consider our relationships continually, and make sure we are doing our part to nourish them so they thrive.

—From *Black Pearls* by Eric V. Copage

What matters is the renewing and long running kinship
seeking common mission, willing work, memory, melody, song.

marriage is an art,
created by the serious, enjoyed by the mature,
watered with morning and evening promises.

those who grow into love
remain anchored
like egyptian architecture and seasonal flowers.

it is afrikan that woman and man join in smile, tears, future.
it is traditional that men and women share expectations,
    celebrations, struggles.
it is legend that the nations start in the family.
it is afrikan that our circle expands.
it is wise that we believe in tomorrows, children, quality.
it is written that our vision will equal the promise.

so that your nation will live and tell your stories accurately,
you must be endless in your loving touch of each other,
your unification is the message,
continuance the answer.

   —"The Union of Two" by Haki R. Madhubuti

Let love be genuine; hate what is evil, hold fast to what is good; love one another with mutual affection; outdo one another in showing honor. Do not lag in zeal, be ardent in spirit, serve the Lord. Rejoice in hope, be patient in suffering, persevere in prayer. Contribute to the needs of the saints; extend hospitality to strangers.

Bless those who persecute you; bless and do not curse them. Rejoice with those who rejoice, weep with those who weep. Live in harmony with one another; do not be haughty, but associate with the lowly; do not claim to be wiser than you are.

—Romans (12:9–16) Holy Bible: New Revised Standard Version

Marriage is the golden ring in a chain whose beginning is a glance and whose ending is Eternity.

—Kahlil Gibran

This beautiful story [of Adam and Eve] tells a fundamental truth about us—that we are made to live in a delicate network of interdependence with one another, with God and with the rest of God's creation. We say in our African idiom: "A person is a person through other persons." A solitary human being is a contradiction in terms. A totally self-sufficient human being is ultimately subhuman. We are made for complementarity. I have gifts that you do not; and you have gifts that I do not. *Voilà!* So we need each other to become fully human.

—From *An African Prayer Book* by Archbishop Desmond Tutu

When you're loving, you're in harmony with life: You feel at one with the most powerful force in the universe, and all the blessings that flow from love are rushing toward you. As Jesus counseled, "Cast your bread [love] on the water, and it shall return to you." Love is the lifespring of our existence. The more love you give, the happier you feel and the more love you will have within you to give.

   —From *In the Spirit* by Susan L. Taylor

And since marriage is an equal partnership, I believe that the woman and the man are equal in power and should by consultation and agreement, mutually decide as to the conduct of the home and the government of the children.

   —Maggie Lena Walker

On February 20, 1977, we were married. . . . The night before, we visited Andrew Young and his wife, Jean, in their suite at the Waldorf-Astoria, where they lived. Andrew was then United States Ambassador to the United Nations. He was also an ordained minister, and he was going to marry us. He and Jean had asked us to come by so they could talk to us about marriage as a sacrament.

That night, Andrew told us about the six people who were to be married by him the next day.

"Six people?" I asked, a little puzzled. "You are marrying six people tomorrow?"

"Yes, and no," Andy replied. "You see, when you and Jeanne get married tomorrow, six people will be involved. With each of you, there are really three persons. First, there is the person you are. Next, there is the person you *think* you are. Then there is the person others think you are. This is true of all marriages, not just yours. And in every marriage, all of these six people have to get along with one another if the contract is to work."

—From *Days of Grace* by Arthur Ashe

One you really love is not around, but with other people. There is the possibility of being jealous. You feel that he is fonder of someone else or that he understands another one better. This is pure selfishness, a kind of love that is not, in fact, genuine. . . . What is required is the feeling of deep, deep love, the kind that wraps itself all around your insides, but does not choke you.

There are loves that choke the love that satisfies. Real love is the love that knows that whenever and wherever you meet again, it's going to be bigger than ever.

—From *Talking to Myself* by Pearl Bailey

≋

As God's chosen ones, holy and beloved, clothe yourselves with compassion, kindness, humility, meekness, and patience. Bear with one another and, if anyone has a complaint against another, forgive each other; just as the Lord has forgiven you, so you also must forgive. Above all, clothe yourselves with love, which binds everything together in perfect harmony. And let the peace of Christ rule in your hearts, to which indeed you were called in the one body. And be thankful.

Colossians (3:12–15) Holy Bible: New Revised Standard Version

◎

I've heard some of the young people laugh about slave love, but they should envy the love which kept mother and father so close together in life, and even held them in death.

—Alonzo Haywood, former enslaved African-American

⌘

What have I learned? That the most special part about being with a woman is to hold them. . . . To have a friend there and touch their hand at the right moment. Just that. . . . There's nothing that I know of that can touch *intimacy*. It's more than sex. Sex is something else, I think. But there's intimacy; you can touch someone's toes with your foot. To be that close. Or just touch someone's cheek or feel their breath on your cheek. And look in someone's eyes and know that you're looking at the truth.

—Richard Pryor, from *Interview*

My parents have always represented, to me, the most surprising alchemy—two such disparate elements mysteriously combined. Mom is a daughter of the Caribbean, raised in Antigua's sun and Leeward winds, well acquainted with the white sand, colorful as only West Indians are and possessor of a broad, cackling laugh, powerful like the hurricanes she knew as a child. Daddy is a son of North Carolina, grown up from fine, dark soil in the shadow of pine trees and tobacco barns, he is strength and wisdom, the keeper of homespun wit and simple, quiet truth. She has taught me how to feel; he has shown me how to think. When I speak to my mother of these differences and marvel aloud at their ability to share a life for over thirty years, she speaks to me of balance. As she sees it, she sits delicately in one brass cup, my father is perched precariously in the other, and, providing the center of the scale is a God of Amazing Grace.

—Patsy Moore, recording artist and poet

Choosing to be in an intimate relationship can be a very exciting and scary process. You're learning how to be part of a couple, while still in the process of being an individual. I think it takes three things to be in a good partnership: (1) respect for each other, (2) shared expectations, and (3) the willingness to be flexible. The love you share with each other will help you openly communicate about these three items.

—From *Girlfriend to Girlfriend* by Julia A. Boyd

I remembered interviewing a thirty-something woman once about how she was able to muster up the will to run marathons. "I can do it because of my husband," she said. "Because he believes I can do anything; he inspires me."

As she spoke my body was engulfed in the most peaceful, joyous warmth I had ever experienced in my life, and I knew without anyone telling me that what I was feeling was pure love. Somehow I had tapped into the love she and her husband felt for each other. Even the palms of my hands and the bottoms of my feet were warm. But more memorable than the warmth was the joy in my heart. I felt a happiness I had never known. It lasted only seconds. I never told anyone, but after feeling it, I knew I wanted that feeling for my life.

—From *Laughing in the Dark* by Patrice Gaines

The healing powers of love are legendary. When we feel we are deeply loved by those around us, we are transformed by that love. We are emboldened by that love to make deep, significant changes in our lives. We become more than just flesh and bone. Our internal wounds no longer bleed or fester. With love, healthy new tissue is formed and old emotional scars vanish.

—From *The Wisdom of the Elders* by Robert Fleming

Make time for one another.
Treat one another with respect.
It's the little things that count.
Learn to trust.

Be willing to share.
Agree to disagree.
Be willing to give in.
Communicate with one another.
Be affectionate.
Share spiritual growth.
Be kind and considerate to one another.
Be easygoing.
Be flexible about growth and change.
Don't cross the line.
Don't let the sun go down on your wrath.
  —Chester Himes

Believe in yourself;
Respect and honor your partner;
Commit to mutual goals; and
Celebrate joint accomplishments.

Honor cultural and religious values;
Empathize and forgive intolerance;
Serve others and give compassion; and
Thank God for your freedom.
  —Advice to the bride and groom from Dr. Marvalene Hughes, Ph.D.,
  President, California State University, Stanislaus

I love roses, but Medgar could never afford to buy me a florist's bouquet. So he did something better: Every year he made a ritual of giving me bare-root roses to plant in our front yard, and eventually, three dozen rosebushes were the envy of our neighbors. Once in a while, Medgar would gather a bouquet, or perhaps just one rose, and hand it to me as he came through the door. It became an unspoken verse of the love between us.

—From *Essence* by Myrlie Evers-Williams

The capacity to love is so tied to being able to be awake, to being able to move out of yourself and be with someone else in a manner that is not about your desire to possess them, but to be with them, to be in union and communion.

—bell hooks

"Do not forsake her, and she will keep you;
    love her, and she will guard you.
The beginning of wisdom is this: Get wisdom,
    and whatever else you get, get insight.
Prize her highly, and she will exalt you;
    she will honor you if you embrace her.
She will place on your head a fair garland;
    she will bestow on you a beautiful crown."

—Proverbs (4:6–9) Holy Bible: New Revised Standard Version

You were born together, and together you shall be
forevermore.

. . . .

Love one another, but make not a bond of love:
Let it rather be a moving sea between the shores of your
souls.
Fill each other's cup but drink not from one cup.
Give one another of your bread but eat not from the
same loaf.
Sing and dance together and be joyous, but let each one of
you be alone,

Even as the strings of a lute are alone though they quiver
with the same music.

Give your hearts, but not into each other's keeping.
For only the hand of Life can contain your hearts.
And stand together yet not too near together:
For the pillars of the temple stand apart,
And the oak tree and the cypress grow not in each other's
shadow.
—From *The Prophet*, by Kahlil Gibran

PRIVATE MOMENTS—JUST FOR THE TWO OF YOU

Let me bathe in the cool waters of your love
—From "Blood on the Fields" by Wynton Marsalis

*T*he passion that a husband and wife feel toward each other is often expressed physically—and naturally—through making love. By consummating your love you are satiating the emotional hunger that burns within. The emotional bond that a man and a woman strengthen through the physical act of making love is unparalleled. This strengthening of the emotional bond is the ultimate gift that a husband and wife can share with each other.

As you read through the selections in this section, you may deem them particularly beautiful and moving, yet too personal to be shared in a formal wedding ceremony. Perhaps you may choose to share these often sensual readings in a more intimate setting where you can verbally and physically express your love, needs, and desires to each other, like on your wedding night. So go ahead, light those vanilla-scented candles, throw on that sexy lingerie, put on your Luther CD for mood music, pop that Dom Pérignon, and let nature take care of the rest. . . .

Last night
we loved as if the gods
had announced only to us
that the sky would fall
while we slept.

We loved
passionately
selflessly
thinking only of pleasure
giving pleasure,

and I knew I would not grieve
if life should end as you held me.

Daybreak.

The sun slid silently
into our room
kissed our faces
and lay softly
in our love bed.

The sky had not fallen.

The earth had not disappeared.

We were alive
to love again.
    —"Loving Again" by Gloria Wade-Gayles

February 19, 1898

My Darling:

I am almost afraid to write to you today for fear that I shall say something that is not quite nice. Dear, your remark about wishing to be asleep in my arms has simply set me afire. I think of you and close my eyes with that sensuous slowness which one adopts when one is being kissed to the fainting point. My whole being palpitates with passion. My fingers tremble, they want to be running through your hair. My face rubs again your velvet cheek. I feel your breath on my lips. I feel your heart throbbing against mine. I hear your whisper—"My Paul," I reach for you—and you are not here.

Dear heart, it is best that we be not together much before we are married. It is a wise Providence that has sent me rushing these thousand miles away as soon as we became engaged and now keeps me chained in another city from you.

I am so glad, though, darling, that it is not a common, vulgar passion that I feel for you. There is something about it that positively uplifts me. Mind and soul are both blended in it, and if my eyes do grow brighter than their wont. If the blood does speed hotter through my veins, if any breath does come in gasps, it is all for my own wife, and no illicit companionship could fill the want, the great yearning which I feel. Now hide your face and blush for the heat of Your Loving Husband.

—From Paul Laurence Dunbar to his wife, Alice Moore Dunbar

February 20, 1898

Dearest husband—I have just been doing what I suppose is a very foolish thing—leaning out of the window in my dressing gown and letting the rain beat on my head. It ached me so badly and I felt so fatigued and feverish that I couldn't resist the temptation. I have been at this desk three hours working like a slave—all school work.

I did not go uptown this afternoon as I had too much to do. Outside a driving rain has been falling for over thirty-six hours without so much as a suspicion of stopping. How I have longed for you! Last night it amounted to a positive ache. You have played me an unfair trick heart of mine; you have so completely woven yourself into the thread of my life until I cannot imagine an existence apart from you.

Paul, my dearest—honestly, it would break my heart were anything to occur to put us apart. Sometimes I catch my breath in a horrible, nameless fear, lest we should be separated.—Your loving wife.

—From Alice Moore Dunbar to her husband, Paul Laurence Dunbar

When I close my eyes . . .

I envision a man and woman committed to empowering and uplifting our people.

I envision a man and a woman overcoming all obstacles placed before them collectively and individually by the support they provide to one another.

I envision a man and a woman living happily as friends, partners, and soul mates loving each other unselfishly and unconditionally.

I envision a man and a woman living with mutual respect and patience, loyalty and honesty.

I envision a man and a woman joined spiritually, metaphysically, and emotionally attaining inner peace and true happiness.

I envision the elders rejoicing in song and dance as they witness a man and a woman pass in righteousness, providing their souls with safe passage into the next millennium with the love and strength of two warriors to endure the ages.

I envision harmony for a man and a woman as they join together as one as they stare into each other's eyes sharing gentle touches, long wet kisses which overwhelm them with passion, exciting and stimulating them as their loins meet and swell, bursting with ecstasy, writhing and wrapping around each other attempting to satisfy the never-ending hunger of their bodies and souls.

I envision a man and a woman smile as they listen to the melodious voices of their children playing and growing with pride as the continuation of the Black family created through the love and faith that God provided them.

I envision a man and a woman on bended knee facing the eastern light in meditation and prayer asking for God's help in keeping their commitments to each other, their families, and their community on the righteous path to everlasting life.

Then when I open my eyes . . .
I see you.

   —"My Vision" by Craig Butler

♦♦♦

Our spirits fly through the universe to join in a joyous union
That comforts us in spite of the distance of our uniqueness
I want to hold you,
wrap my arms around you,
whisper sweet somethings in your ear.
Lick your lips, kiss your eyebrows.
Taste your nectar.
This hunger I feel for you has taken away my appetite for
    bodily nourishment.
I melt at the thought of being near you,
at the touch of your hand on mine,
at the sound of your rough voice.
Feed my hungry body.
Quench the thirst of my desire with your mere presence.
Satiate my spirit with sustenance from your soul,
Your body touches mine,

            y s
          g e
        r s
      e i
    n R
  E

We come together
In mind, body, soul, and spirit.
Hands and hearts entwined by love.
I want to promise you the moon . . . the stars . . . a galaxy of
    love,
I can only give you my Self . . .
Today . . . tomorrow and
Tomorrow . . . and tomorrow . . .
I look into your eyes and see reflected my beauty,
my love,

my sweetness,
and my light,
that grow with each passing day.
Your gentle acceptance enables me to thrive,
To approach the tempting vistas my soul yearns to explore,
Vast horizons beckon endlessly . . .
Yet my connection to you is solidly ephemeral.
As is the silver cord that binds this body
to that ceaselessly searching soul.
Stay with me.
Let us share our joys, our sorrows, our feelings.
Let nothing that comes between us separate us.
Our belief in our fidelity allows us to remain in a state of bliss,
The seldom found condition that binds two lives . . .
together . . .
eternally . . .

   —"Life Partners" by Monique Jellerette deJongh and Cassandra Marshall Cato-Louis

Darling, my darling, my heart is
on the wing,
   It flies to thee this morning like a bird,
Like happy birds in springtime my spirits soar and sing,
   The same sweet song thine ears have often heard.

The sun is in my window, the shadow on the lea,
   The wind is moving in the branches green,
And all my life, my darling, is turning unto thee,
   And kneeling at thy feet, my own, my queen.

The golden bells are ringing across the distant hill,
   Their merry peals come to me soft and clear,
But in my heart's deep chapel all incense-filled and still
   A sweeter bell is sounding for thee, dear.

The bell of love invites thee to come and seek the shrine

   Whose altar is erected unto thee,
The offerings, the sacrifice, the prayers, the chants are thine,
   And I, my love, thy humble priest will be.
   —"Morning Song of Love" by Paul Laurence Dunbar

I give you love and joy and all good things
That summer brings:
Leaf in a sympathetic breeze, a dawn
To wish upon,

Cool grasses' dew, benevolence of rain,
Release from pain,
Burst of a blossom, sustenance of prayer,
The sun's first flare.

First breath of dawn, the sky's first blue I bring,
A song to sing,
And peace beside a slow and sinuous stream
Where you can dream.

My days' first thought, my nights' last consciousness,
My dreamed caress,
Rebirth of joy and love each day anew—
These are for you.
    —"Morning Song" by Naomi Long Madgett

Melodious, seductive
    You travel into the
galaxies of my
    life

Stirring moods, feelings
unexplored

    sounds

Powerful like the
    summer sun

    yet

soothing as the
morning mist

You leave me in
    total
        bliss.
    —"Universal Queen" by Tommye Lee Ray

I

In the evening, love returns,
　　Like a wand'rer 'cross the sea;
In the evening, love returns

　　With a violet for me;
In the evening, life's a song,
　　And the fields are full of green;
All the stars are golden crowns,
　　And the eye of God is keen.

II

In the evening, sorrow dies
　　With the setting of the sun;
In the evening, joy begins,
　　When the course of mirth is done;
In the evening, kisses sweet
　　Droop upon the passion vine;
In the evening comes your voice:
　　"I am yours, and you are mine."
　　—"In the Evening" by Fenton Johnson

The perfume of your body dulls my sense.
　　I want nor wine nor weed; your breath alone
Suffices. In this moment rare and tense
　　I worship at your breast. The flower is blown,
The saffron petals tempt my amorous mouth,
　　The yellow heart is radiant now with dew
Soft-scented, redolent of my loved South;
　　O flower of love! I give myself to you.

Uncovered on your couch of figured green,
  Here let us linger indivisible.
The portals of your sanctuary unseen
  Receive my offering, yielding unto me.
Oh, with our love the night is warm and deep!
  The air is sweet, my flower, and sweet the flute
Whose music lulls our burning brain to sleep,
  While we lie loving, passionate and mute.
  —"Flower of Love" by Claude McKay

In your presence I rediscovered my name
My name that was hidden under the pain of separation
I rediscovered the eyes no longer veiled with fever
And your laughter like a flame piercing the shadows
Has revealed Africa to me beyond the snows of yesterday
Ten years my love
With days of illusions and shattered ideas
And sleep made restless with alcohol
The suffering that burdens today with the taste of tomorrow
And that turns love into a boundless river
In your presence I have rediscovered the memory of my blood
And necklaces of laughter hung around our days
Days sparkling with ever new joys.
  —"Your Presence" by David Diop (Senegal)

Come when the nights are bright with stars
Or come when the moon is mellow;
Come when the sun his golden bars
Drops on the hay-field yellow.
Come in the twilight soft and gray,
Come in the night or come in the day,
Come, O Love, whene'er you may,
And you are welcome, welcome.

You are sweet, O Love, dear Love,
You are soft as the nesting dove.
Come to my heart and bring it rest
As the bird flies home to its welcome nest.

Come when my heart is full of grief
Or when my heart is merry;
Come with the falling of the leaf
Or with the redd'ning cherry.
Come when the year's first blossom blows,
Come when the summer gleams and glows,
Come with the winter's drifting snows,
And you are welcome, welcome.
    —"Invitation to Love" by Paul Laurence Dunbar

I love you for your brownness,
And the rounded darkness of your breast,
I love you for the breaking sadness in your voice
And shadows where your wayward eyelids rest.

Something of old forgotten queens
Lurks in the lithe abandon of your walk
And something of the shackled slave
Sobs in the rhythm of your talk.

Oh, little brown girl, born for sorrow's mate,
Keep all you have of queenliness,
Forgetting that you once were slave,
And let your full lips laugh at Fate!
    —"To a Dark Girl" by Gwendolyn B. Bennett

You are like a warm dark dusk
In the middle of June-time
When the first violets
Have almost forgotten their names
And the deep red roses bloom.

You are like a warm dark dusk
In the middle of June-time
Before the hot nights of summer
Burn white with stars.
    —"Young Negro Girl" by Langston Hughes

Thoughts run tonight
racing into dark corners
startle me with
their brittleness
blinding
with their insistent bright
edge

Madness propels them
over and over again—
variations on the same theme

But I will drive east
to the river at daybreak
where I have my beginnings,
will lose myself in the center
of dawn

Having roots in that place,
I will follow the streak of red
that cuts the sky
When light claims
the earth,
I will reach out and touch
your coolness invisible
without shadow
and bright as a copper coin
in sunlight

I will take you into my madness
and hold you in full bloom
　　—"One More for Love" by Pinkie Gordon Lane

clouds fill the sky
the breeze is cool
work a demanding task

i walk

my mind is relaxed
my body, remembering
the morning after love

a feeling fills my heart
like a cup of calm black
mist, refreshing

i walk

a new day, remembering
for a short spell
your embrace.

life trying to take on new
meaning, a dirty world reaching
for lustre.

I smell chrysanthemums from
tomorrow months.

and blinding rain drops smell
of perfume
on the morning after . . . love.

i walk.
   —"The Morning After . . . Love" by Kattie M. Cumbo

First thing in the morning seeking
   some relief; can I tell you
   of a dream that wasn't a dream
at all—

Can I tell you how I passed the night
   mind screaming for day light;
   can I tell you of a tortured
conscience.

This should have been dream
   but no, you were standing before me
   in your magnificence, close enough
for me to whisper in your ear—

To smell the fragrance of your skin,
   to see it tremble ever slightly
   wanted to reach out, touch you but knew
you were an illusion—

Closed my eyes, breathed you in
   my body came alive; the house was still,
   dark; could hear the wooden floors
creaking—

Sounds of night echoing off bay windows
   where I lay; wanted you with a fire that
   singed my skin, begged for daylight
there was no relief—

Wanted to devour you: mind, body & soul
   wanted your essence: be part of you,
   become you, nothing short of that would do
no sleep, no relief—

Now in day light: coolness of the early morn,
   in the breakfast nook, door open,
   morning breeze your kiss & fingers across
my face:

I need but close my eyes, transported
   back in time, a train station, where for the
   briefest moment the world stopped; and I
kissed the world's most splendid lips
      —"Phantom XIV Enraptured" by Clyde A. Wray

To clasp you now and feel your head close-pressed,
Scented and warm against my beating breast;

To whisper soft and quivering your name,
And drink the passion burning in your frame;

To lie at full length, taut, with cheek to cheek,
And tease your mouth with kisses till you speak

Love words, mad words, dream words, sweet senseless words,
Melodious like notes of mating birds;

To hear you ask if I shall love always,
And myself answer: Till the end of days;

To feel your easeful sigh of happiness
When on your trembling lips I murmur: Yes;

It is so sweet. We know it is not true.
What matters it? The night must shed her dew.

We know it is not true, but it is sweet—
The poem with this music is complete.
      —"Romance" by Claude McKay

♥

I wish I could be
the water of your bath
    I would surround you
    with mellow warmth
    liquid love
like a frolicking/childish wave
on the sandy shore
    I would dash and break
    upon the firmness of your body
    engulf and moisten
    the places I dream of
    —From "Water of Your Bath" by Ahmasi

This morning I visited the place where we lay
like animals
O pride be forgotten
And how the moon bathed our savage nudity in purity
And your hands touched mine in a silken caress
And our beings were cleansed as though by wine.
    Then you stroked my breast
And through love I shed the tears of my womb
O sweet fluid spilled in the name of love
O love
O sweet of mine existence
Your sigh of content as your lips touched my soul
O joy shared by the wilderness
O gentle breeze
O fireflies that hovered over our nest in protective harmony
How I yearn
I feel you here again with me.

See how the flowers, the grass, even the little shrubs have
   bloomed
Even as I bloomed under the warmth of your breath
And now they look at me; unashamed
For they have been washed and watered by the love of your
   loins
I stretch and sigh in warm contemplation
For tonight I shall again possess you
In me, I shall be content of all you render
On account of love
Under the stars I shall drink the whisperings of your body
Speak again to the depths of my sensibility
Tree of my life
Peaceful meadows
Cow dares not moo here
Ruler of the night
Lord dynamo
Let me not disturb your peace
But let me lie with you again
Be silent O silence
Love has found its awakening
   —"This Morning" by Kristina Rungano (Zimbabwe)

you come to me
during the cool hours
of the day bringing
the sun; if you come
at midnight, or at two
in the morning, you come
always bringing the sun;
the taste of your sweetness
permeates my lips and my hair
with the lingering sweetness of Harlem
with the lingering sweetness of Africa
with the lingering sweetness of freedom;
woman, eye want to see
your breast brown and bared,
your nippled eyes staring,
aroused-hard and lovely;
woman, eye want to see
the windows of your suffering
washed clean of this terrible pain
we endure together;
woman, eye want to see
your song filled with joy,
feel the beat of your laughter;
woman, black beautiful woman,
eye want to see
your black graceful body
covered with the sweat of our love
with your dancer's steps to music
moving rhythmically, panther like
across the African veldt;
woman, eye want to see you
naked, always in your natural beauty;

woman, eye want to see you
proud; in your native land
   —"You Come to Me" by Quincy Troupe

I want to die while you love me,
   While yet you hold me fair,
While laughter lies upon my lips
   And lights are in my hair.

I want to die while you love me
   And bear to that still bed
Your kisses turbulent, unspent
   To warm me when I'm dead.

I want to die while you love me
   Oh, who would care to live
Till love has nothing more to ask
   And nothing more to give!

I want to die while you love me
   And never, never see
The glory of this perfect day
   Grow dim or cease to be!
   —"I Want to Die While You Love Me" by Georgia Douglas Johnson

Naked woman, black woman
Clothed with your colour which is life, with your form which is
    beauty!
In your shadow I have grown up; the gentleness of your hands
    was laid over my eyes.
And now, high up on the sun-baked pass, at the heart of
    summer, at the heart of noon, I come upon you, my
    Promised Land,
And your beauty strikes me to the heart like the flash of an eagle.

Naked woman, dark woman
Firm-fleshed ripe fruit, sombre raptures of black wine, mouth
    making lyrical my mouth
Savannah stretching to clear horizons, savannah shuddering
    beneath the East Wind's eager caresses
Carved tom-tom, taut tom-tom, muttering under the
    Conqueror's fingers
Your solemn contralto voice is the spiritual song of the Beloved.

Naked woman, dark woman
Oil that no breath ruffles, calm oil on the athlete's flanks, on
    the flanks of the Princes of Mali
Gazelle-limbed in Paradise, pearls are stars on the night of your
    skin
Delights of the mind, the glinting of red gold against your
    watered skin
Under the shadow of your hair, my care is lightened by the
    neighbouring suns of your eyes.

Naked woman, black woman
I sing your beauty that passes, the form that I fix in the Eternal,
Before jealous Fate turn you to ashes to feed the roots of life.
    —"Black Woman" by Léopold Sédar Senghor (Senegal)

Reaffirmations of Our Love

Because you love me I have much achieved.
—From "Encouraged" by Paul Laurence Dunbar

It's amazing how time brings couples closer together. I never thought that I could love my husband any more than on our wedding day. But with each passing day my love for him grows more intense, passionate, and steadfast. Our love is anchored in a sea of experience that continues to survive many turbulent storms—some forecasted, some unforeseen. But with each storm that we weather, our anchor of love becomes more entrenched in the sea of life experiences rather than eroding from the powerful waves that constantly attempt to dislodge it. And this is what bonds us together—all those incredible years of trials and tribulations that test the strength of our love.

The passages assembled in this section are ideal for married couples who want to renew their wedding vows after many years together. If you are blessed with children, having each child recite a passage during the reaffirmation ceremony is a beautiful way for the entire family to cherish this most memorable celebration of love.

For those of you just beginning your married lives together, the following passages can serve as a reminder of how important it is to

rededicate yourselves to the relationship and each other on a regular basis. Perhaps you can start a tradition as a couple that every five years you will reaffirm your love and devotion to one another by having a reaffirmation ceremony.

Only death can rob me of my will to love the one I love:
—Joshua Henry Jones

How good it is to let our memory wander
And travel back across the fruitful years
To count how many miles we've walked together!
On pinnacles of dreams, through vales of tears,
Along the level ground of every day
   We've made our way.

In sickness and in health, in joy and sadness,
Together, side by side, sunshine or shade,
   We've worked toward common goals, found satisfaction
   In all the hours of which our years are made.
   All things were possible because we shared,
     Because we cared.

And after many years, we still hold dearest
Of all life's blessings anywhere on earth
The trust and honor that we give each other,
The love that gave our other blessings birth.
Praise be that I am yours by plan divine,
   That you are mine!
—"Anniversary Song" by Naomi Long Madgett

i shall save my poems
for the winter of my dreams
i look forward to huddling
in my rocker with my life
i wonder what i'll contemplate
lovers—certainly those
i can remember
and knowing my life
you'll be there

you'll be there in the cold
like a Siamese on my knee
proud purring when you let me stroke you

you'll be there in the rain
like an umbrella over my head
sheltering me from the damp mist

you'll be there in the dark
like a lighthouse in the fog
seeing me through troubled waters

you'll be there in the sun
like coconut oil on my back
to keep me from burning

i shall save a special poem
for you to say
you always made me smile
and even though i cried sometimes
you said i will not let you
down

my rocker and i on winter's porch
will never be sad if you're gone

the winter's cold has been stored
against
you will always be
there
   —"You Are There" by Nikki Giovanni

When buffeted and beaten by life's storms,
When by the bitter cares of life oppressed,
I want no surer haven than your arms,
I want no sweeter heaven than your breast.

When over my life's way there falls the blight
Of sunless days, and nights of starless skies;
Enough for me, the calm and steadfast light
That softly shines within your loving eyes.

The world, for me, and all the world can hold
Is circled by your arms; for me there lies,
Within the lights and shadows of your eyes,
The only beauty that is never old.
   —"Beauty That Is Never Old" by James Weldon Johnson

Susan and I draw inspiration from couples who have remained happily married for many years. And so it was a particular joy for us to spend an afternoon and evening with Ossie Davis and Ruby Dee talking about their relationship, a conversation that eventually became an article for *Essence* magazine. Speaking of their forty-something-year marriage, Ruby, in her wise and poetic way, noted, "The wedding is a fact; the marriage is a process, and it's ongoing."

Tapping into an older, more significant meaning of the word "marriage," Ruby contrasts the ritual of the event—the marriage ceremony—with the ongoing work of integrating two lives into a whole that is greater than the sum of its parts. We've seen this in couples who can finish each other's sentences, who know each other so intimately they seem to think each other's thoughts, who even begin to look alike. The process that results in such a union of two souls is a paradigm for the ultimate union of every soul in God and is a step toward that union. And it is for that reason that marriage has been regarded as sacred by all cultures throughout time, and that ceremonies solemnizing the event have invoked the gods to witness our commitments to love—that is, to sacrifice for, do for, and think of someone other than ourselves.

—From *Confirmation* by Khephra Burns and Susan L. Taylor

Through storm or calm your vessel has swept on;
Bravely and well your life work has been done,
Till now, you wait the setting of life's sun.
Five full decades have quickly passed away
Since lapsing Autumn hailed your wedding day.
You cared not then that Summer days were fled,

And frosty rime the landscape overspread,
Your hearts were warm and could defy the frost,
Not all caloric have they, as yet, lost;
For true love, married, seldom will grow cold,
Though step and feature tell we're growing old.
Love's flame still burns, with soft and mellow light,
And far from fading, groweth yet more bright.
It is a marvel in these divorce days
Of transient unions, matrimonial strays,
That Thomas and Annette should stick together
For fifty years, in every sort of weather.

   —From "A Golden Wedding Poem" by Reverend L. Burleigh, written
   in celebration of the fiftieth anniversary of Thomas and Annette
   Lathrop, who were married in 1830

My monkey-wrench man is my sweet patootie;
the lover of my life, my youth and age.
My heart belongs to him and to him only;
the children of my flesh are his and bear his rage
Now grown to years advancing through the dozens
the honeyed kiss, the lips of wine and fire
fade blissfully into the distant years of yonder
but all my days of Happiness and wonder
are cradled in his arms and eyes entire.
They carry us under the waters of the world
out past the starposts of a distant planet
And creeping through the seaweed of the ocean
they tangle us with ropes and yarn of memories
where we have been together, you and I.

   —"Love Song for Alex, 1979" by Margaret Walker Alexander

Love me. I care not what the
　　circling years
　　　　To me may do.
If, but in spite of time and tears,
　　　　You prove but true.

Love me—albeit grief shall dim
　　mine eyes,
　　　　And tears bedew,
I shall not e'en complain, for then
　　my skies
　　　　Shall still be blue.

Love me, and though the winter
　　snow shall pile,
　　　　And leave me chill,
Thy passion's warmth shall make
　　for me, meanwhile,
　　　　A sun-kissed hill.

And when the days have lengthened into years,
　　　　And I grow old,
Oh, spite of pains and griefs and
　　cares and fears,
　　　　Grow thou not cold.

Then hand and hand we shall pass
　　up the hill,
　　　　I say not down;
That twain go up, of love, who've
　　loved their fill,—
　　　　To gain love's crown.

Love me, and let my life take up

thine own,
    As sun the dew.
Come, sit, my queen, for in my
    heart a throne
      Awaits for you!
    —"Love's Apotheosis" by Paul Laurence Dunbar

When you see me leavin,
    Hang yo haid and cry, Lawd, Lawd,
When you see me leavin,
    Hang yo haid and cry.
Gonna Love you
    Til the day I die.
    —Traditional folk song

Enjoy life with the wife whom you love, all the days of your vain life that are given you under the sun, because that is your portion in life and in your toil at which you toil under the sun.
    —Ecclesiastes (9:9) Holy Bible: New Revised Standard Version

When you loved me
you not only nursed
and nourished me
to a fresh wholesomeness,
you taught me
how to laugh
even as tears scorched
my burning throat.

You gave me everything
a fortune
that gave birth
to our present
treasure bank
and in time taught me
to deposit
not to take all the time.

Look how rich we are
together now!

Hold here, feel
how my heart dances with sheer joy
listen to that new rhythm you have created
those thrilling, caressing blood currents
that flow through my whole being
bringing home a million messages
telling me how I truly belong.
   —"Look How Rich We Are Together" by Mícere M.G. Mũgo

ACKNOWLEDGMENTS

In researching this book, it was a great reading pleasure to devour the volumes listed below. So often I'd find myself sitting in the library after hours had passed lost in the authors' magical words of love. If time allows, I can only hope you have the same opportunity to explore these sources at your library or bookstore and discover for yourself the wonder of our African-American literary heritage. I offer peace and blessings to these authors for their inspiration.

I gratefully acknowledge the following sources, which are included in this book (in the order of appearance):

John (4:16–19): From The New Revised Standard Version of the Bible (Nashville: Thomas Nelson, 1989). Copyright © 1989 by the Division of Christian Education of the National Council of the Churches of Christ in the USA. Used by permission. All rights reserved.

Terry McMillan: From *How Stella Got Her Groove Back* by Terry McMillan (New York: Viking, 1996). Copyright © 1996 by Terry McMillan.

Nikki Giovanni: "Love Is" from *Love Poems* by Nikki Giovanni (New

York: William Morrow & Company, 1997). Copyright © 1968, 1997 by Nikki Giovanni. Reprinted by permission of William Morrow & Company, Inc.

Gwendolyn Brooks: "To Be in Love" from *Blacks* by Gwendolyn Brooks (Chicago: Third World Press, 1991). Copyright © 1991 by Gwendolyn Brooks. Reprinted by permission of Third World Press.

Kahlil Gibran: Excerpt from *The Earth Gods* by Kahlil Gibran (New York: Alfred A. Knopf, 1931). Copyright © 1920 by Kahlil Gibran and renewed 1948 by the Administrators C.T.A. of Kahlil Gibran Estate and Mary G. Gibran. Reprinted by permission of Alfred A. Knopf, Inc.

Joseph S. Cotter Jr.: "Love" from *The Band of Gideon and Other Lyrics* by Joseph S. Cotter Jr. (Boston: The Cornhill Company, 1918). Copyright © 1918 by The Cornhill Company.

Nikki Giovanni: "The World Is Not a Pleasant Place to Be" from *My House* by Nikki Giovanni (New York: William Morrow & Company, 1972). Copyright © 1972 by Nikki Giovanni. Reprinted by permission of William Morrow & Company, Inc.

Samuel Washington Johnson: Reprinted from *The Black Family in Slavery and Freedom: 1750–1925* by Herbert G. Gutman (New York: Pantheon Books, 1976). Copyright © 1976 by Herbert G. Gutman.

George Moses Horton: "The Powers of Love" from *The Poetical Works of George M. Horton, The Colored Bard of North Carolina* by George M. Horton (Hillsborough, NC: D. Heartt, 1845).

Pinkie Gordon Lane: "Lyric: I Am Looking at Music" from *Girl at the Window* by Pinkie Gordon Lane (Baton Rouge: Louisiana State University Press, 1991). Copyright © 1991 by Pinkie Gordon Lane. Reprinted by permission of the author.

Countee Cullen: "Love's Way" by Countee Cullen from *Copper Sun* by Countee Cullen (New York: Harper & Brothers, 1927). Copyright © 1927 by Harper & Brothers; copyright renewed 1955 by Ida M. Cullen. Reprinted by permission of GRM Associates, Inc., Agents for the Estate of Ida M. Cullen.

Colin L. Powell: From *My American Journey* by Colin L. Powell with

Terry McMillan: From *How Stella Got Her Groove Back* by Terry McMillan (New York: Viking, 1996). Copyright © 1996 by Terry McMillan.

James Weldon Johnson: "The Awakening" from *Fifty Years & Other Poems* by James Weldon Johnson (Boston: The Cornhill Company, 1917).

John (4:7–12): From The New Revised Standard Version of the Bible (Nashville: Thomas Nelson, 1989). Copyright © 1989 by the Division of Christian Education of the National Council of the Churches of Christ in the USA. Used by permission. All rights reserved.

Nikki Giovanni: "You Came, Too" from *Black Feeling, Black Talk, Black Judgement* by Nikki Giovanni (New York: William Morrow & Company, 1970). Copyright © 1968, 1970 by Nikki Giovanni. Reprinted by permission of William Morrow & Company, Inc.

Annette Jones White: "Lovers' Dialogue" by Annette Jones White is an original poem published by permission of the author. Copyright © 1997 by Annette Jones White.

Claude McKay: "Summer Morn in New Hampshire" from *Selected Poems of Claude McKay* by Claude McKay (New York: Bookman Associates, 1953). Copyright © 1981 by Harcourt Brace.

Nathaniel I. Twitt: "Dream about Me" by Nathaniel I. Twitt reprinted from *Ebony Rhythm*, edited by Beatrice M. Murphy (The Exposition Press, 1948). Copyright © 1948 by The Exposition Press.

Georgia Holloway Jones: "Enchantment" by Georgia Holloway Jones reprinted from *Ebony Rhythm*, edited by Beatrice M. Murphy (The Exposition Press, 1948). Copyright © 1948 by The Exposition Press.

Stephany: "Moving Deep" from *Moving Deep* by Stephany (Detroit: Broadside Press, 1969). Copyright © 1969 by Stephany. Reprinted by permission of Broadside Press.

Sonia Sanchez: "We Can Be" from *It's a New Day* by Sonia Sanchez (Detroit: Broadside Press, 1971). Copyright © 1971 by Sonia Sanchez. Reprinted by permission of the author.

Joseph S. Cotter Jr.: "Poem #63" from *The Band of Gideon and Other Lyrics* by Joseph S. Cotter Jr. (Boston: The Cornhill Company, 1918). Copyright © 1918 by The Cornhill Company.

Patsy Moore: This original tribute to her mother and father is published by permission of the author.

Julia A. Boyd: Excerpt from *Girlfriend to Girlfriend* by Julia A. Boyd (New York: Dutton, 1995). Copyright © 1995 by Julia A. Boyd.

Patrice Gaines: Excerpt from *Laughing in the Dark* by Patrice Gaines (New York: Doubleday, 1994). Copyright © 1994 by Patrice Gaines.

Robert Fleming: Excerpt from *The Wisdom of the Elders* by Robert Fleming (New York: Ballantine, 1996). Copyright © 1996 by Robert Fleming.

Chester Himes: Reprinted from *The Nubian Wedding Book* by Ingrid Sturgis (New York: Crown Publishers, 1997). Copyright © 1997 by Ingrid Sturgis.

Marvalene Hughes: Advice to the bride and groom is published by permission of the author.

Myrlie Evers-Williams: Excerpt from "Remembering Medgar" from *Essence*, February 1986.

Proverbs (4:6–9): From The New Revised Standard Version of the Bible (Nashville: Thomas Nelson, 1989). Copyright © 1989 by the Division of Christian Education of the National Council of the Churches of Christ in the USA. Used by permission. All rights reserved.

Kahlil Gibran: Excerpt from *The Prophet* by Kahlil Gibran (New York: Alfred A. Knopf, 1923). Copyright © 1923 by Kahlil Gibran. Renewal copyright © 1951 by Administrators C.T.A. of Kahlil Gibran Estate, and Mary G. Gibran. Reprinted by permission of Alfred A. Knopf, Inc.

Gloria Wade-Gayles: "Loving Again" from *Anointed to Fly* (New York: Harlem River Press, 1991). Copyright © 1991 by Glorie Wade-Gayles. Reprinted by permission of the author.

Paul Laurence Dunbar: From "The Letters of Paul and Alice Dunbar" by Eugene Wesley Metcalf, Ph.D. dissertation, University of California, Irvine, 1973. In *Language and Literature, Modern* (Ann Arbor, Michigan: University Microfilms, A Xerox Company).

Alice Moore Dunbar: From "The Letters of Paul and Alice Dunbar" by Eugene Wesley Metcalf, Ph.D. dissertation, University of California,

Irvine, 1973. In *Language and Literature, Modern* (Ann Arbor, Michigan: University Microfilms, A Xerox Company).

Craig Butler: "My Vision" by Craig Butler is an original poem published by permission of the author. Copyright © 1997 by Craig Butler.

Monique Jellerette deJongh and Cassandra Marshall Cato-Louis: "Life Partners" from *How to Marry a Black Man* by Monique Jellerette deJongh and Cassandra Marshall Cato-Louis (New York: Doubleday, 1996). Copyright © 1996 by Monique Jellerette deJongh and Cassandra Marshall Cato-Louis. Reprinted by permission of Doubleday, a division of Bantam Doubleday Dell Publishing Group, Inc.

Paul Laurence Dunbar: "Morning Song of Love" from *The Complete Poems of Paul Laurence Dunbar* by Paul Laurence Dunbar (New York: Dodd, Mead and Company, 1905).

Naomi Long Madgett: "Morning Song" from *Star by Star* by Naomi Long Madgett (Harlo, 1956; Evenill, 1970). Copyright © 1956, 1970 by Naomi Long Madgett. Reprinted by permission of the author.

Tommye Lee Ray: "Universal Queen" by Tommye Lee Ray is an original poem published by permission of the author.

Fenton Johnson: "In the Evening" from *A Little Dreaming* by Fenton Johnson (Chicago: Peterson Linotyping Company, 1913). Copyright © 1913 by Fenton Johnson.

Claude McKay: "Flower of Love" from *Selected Poems of Claude McKay* by Claude McKay (New York: Bookman Associates, 1953). Copyright © 1981 by Harcourt Brace.

David Diop: "Your Presence" reprinted from *Modern Poetry from Africa* edited by Gerald Moore and Ulli Beier (Middlesex, UK, Penguin Books, 1966). Copyright © 1963 by Gerald Moore and Ulli Beier.

Paul Laurence Dunbar: "Invitation to Love" from *The Complete Poems of Paul Laurence Dunbar* by Paul Laurence Dunbar (New York: Dodd, Mead and Company, 1905).

Gwendolyn B. Bennett: "To a Dark Girl" published in *Opportunity 5* (1927). Reprinted by permission of the Schomberg Center for Research in Black Culture, New York Library.

Langston Hughes: "Young Negro Girl" from *Collected Poems* by Langston Hughes (New York: Alfred A. Knopf, 1994). Copyright © 1994 by the Estate of Langston Hughes. Reprinted by permission of Alfred A. Knopf, Inc.

Pinkie Gordon Lane: "One More for Love" from *Girl at the Window* by Pinkie Gordon Lane (Baton Rouge: Louisiana State University Press, 1991). Copyright © 1991 by Pinkie Gordon Lane. Reprinted by permission of the author.

Kattie M. Cumbo: "The Morning After ... Love" from *Nine Black Poets*, edited by R. Baird Shuman (Durham, NC: Moore Publishing Company, 1968). Reprinted by permission of Moore Publishing Company and R. Baird Shuman.

Clyde A. Wray: "Phantom XIV Enraptured" is an original poem published by permission of the author.

Claude McKay: "Romance" from *Selected Poems of Claude McKay* by Claude McKay (New York: Bookman Associates, 1953). Copyright © 1981 by Harcourt Brace.

Ahmasi: Excerpt from "Water of Your Bath" by Ahmasi, was originally published in *Essence* magazine, May 1977, and reprinted in *I Hear a Symphony* by Paula Woods & Felix Liddell (New York: Doubleday, 1994). Copyright © 1971 by Ahmasi. Reprinted by permission of the author.

Kristina Rungano (Zimbabwe): "This Morning" by Kristina Rungano from *A Storm Is Brewing* (Zimbabwe: Zimbabwe Publishing House, 1984) reprinted from *The Heinemann Book of African Women's Poetry* edited by Stella and Frank Chipasula (Oxford: Heinemann, 1995). Copyright © 1995 by Stella and Frank Chipasula.

Quincy Troupe: "You Come to Me" from *Embryo* by Quincy Troupe (Barlenmir House, 1972). Copyright © 1972 by Quincy Troupe. Reprinted by permission of author.

Georgia Douglas Johnson: "I Want to Die While You Love Me" by Georgia Douglas Johnson from *Caroling Dusk* edited by Countee Cullen (New York: Harper & Brothers, 1927) and reprinted from *Trouble the Water: 250 Years of African-American Poetry* edited by Jerry W. Ward Jr. (New York: Mentor, 1997). Copyright © 1997 by Jerry W. Ward Jr.

Léopold Sédar Senghor (Senegal): "Black Woman" by Léopold Sédar Senghor (translated from the French by John Reed and Clive Wake) and reprinted from *Voices from Twentieth-Century Africa,* edited by Chinweizu (London: Faber & Faber Ltd, 1988). Copyright © 1988 by Chinweizu.

Naomi Long Madgett: "Anniversary Song" by Naomi Long Madgett. Copyright © 1987 by Naomi Long Madgett. Reprinted by permission of the author.

Nikki Giovanni: "You Are There" from *Cotton Candy on a Rainy Day* by Nikki Giovanni (New York: William Morrow & Company, 1978). Copyright © 1978 by Nikki Giovanni. Reprinted by permission of William Morrow & Company, Inc.

James Weldon Johnson: "Beauty That Is Never Old" from *Fifty Years & Other Poems* by James Weldon Johnson (Boston: The Cornhill Company, 1917).

Khephra Burns and Susan L. Taylor: From *Confirmation: The Spiritual Wisdom that Has Shaped Us* edited by Khephra Burns and Susan L. Taylor, editor (New York: Doubleday, 1997). Copyright © 1997 by Khephra Burns and Susan L. Taylor. Used by permission of Doubleday, a division of Bantam Doubleday Dell Publishing Group, Inc.

Reverend L. Burleigh: From "A Golden Wedding Poem" by Reverend L. Burleigh, November 25, 1880. Reprinted by permission of Brown University Library.

Margaret Walker Alexander: "Love Song for Alex, 1979" from *This Is My Century: New and Collected Poems* by Margaret Walker Alexander. Copyright © 1989 by Margaret Walker Alexander. Reprinted by permission of the University of Georgia Press.

Paul Laurence Dunbar: "Love's Apotheosis" from *The Complete Poems of Paul Laurence Dunbar* by Paul Laurence Dunbar (New York: Dodd, Mead and Company, 1905).

Ecclesiastes (9:9): From The New Revised Standard Version of the Bible

AUTHOR'S NOTE

My deepest thanks and gratitude are extended to the following people who made this book a reality. Thank you Jennifer Moore, my editor, for having the vision to create this collection as well as providing me with the latitude to develop it as I wished. Thank you Deirdre Mullane for suggesting to your Dutton associates that I edit this collection. As always, thank you to my enthusiastic and vivacious agent, Meg Ruley—a constant source of inspiration (and the good folks at the Jane Rotrosen Agency). Thanks to the people at Dutton who brought this book to you. A heartfelt thanks to all of the permissions people at the various publishing companies for your help. Thank you to many of the contributors from my previous book *My Mother Had a Dream* for providing material for this collection, including some from my role models Pinkie Gordon Lane, Naomi Long Madgett, Sonia Sanchez, and Annette Jones White.

Thank you Professor Lynn Bolles for filling my head during my sophomore year at Bowdoin College with the many wonders of the African diaspora. Thank you to my mother and father, Odeline and Charles Townes, who taught me through example that marriage is

comprised of two equal partners who must persevere no matter what potholes they drive over on life's road. No words can begin to express my gratitude to Gail and Glenn Matthews for creating their son and my husband, Scott Matthews—Scott is my eternal soul mate as well as the love of my life and all my future lives hereafter.

Finally, thank you Scott for finding and nurturing the writer in me. God has given me the greatest gift in the universe—you as my shepherd.

About the Author

Tamara Alexandra Nikuradse is a graduate of Bowdoin College and the Graduate School of Business Administration at Harvard University. She has coauthored eight books with her husband, Scott Matthews, including the best-selling *To the Man I Love: Thank You for Being Mine* and *To the Woman I Love: Thank You for Being Mine*. Tamara's last book, published by Plume in 1997, *My Mother Had a Dream: African-American Women Share Their Mothers' Words of Wisdom,* is a smart, sassy, and inspirational collection of homespun wit and timeless wisdom handed down from one generation of African-American mothers to the next generation of African-American daughters.

Tamara lives in the Boston area with her husband and their three cats, Lisa, Black Beauty, and Dog Meat. Tamara can be reached at 304 Newbury St., No. 430, Boston, MA 02115 or at nikuradse@aol.com.

Index

Walker, Margaret, 1
White, Annette Jones, 36–37, 65
Wilson, August, 97
Wray, Clyde A., 132–33

Wright, Jeremiah A., Jr., 87

Yerby, Frank, 42